TIMEFC
HORSES TO FOLLOW

2008/09 JUMPS SEASON

CONTENTS

ISBN 978 1 901570 71 7   Price £6.95

Printed and bound by the
Charlesworth Group,
Wakefield, UK 01924 204830

Timeform's Fifty To Follow

Timeform's Fifty To Follow, carefully chosen by members of Timeform's editorial staff, are listed below with their respective page numbers. A selection of ten (marked in orange) is made for those who prefer a smaller list

Timeform's Fifty To Follow in 2008/09

The form summary for each horse is shown after its age, colour, sex and pedigree. The summary shows the distance, the state of the going and where the horse finished in each of its races since the start of the 2007/8 season. Performances are in chronological sequence with the date of its last race shown at the end.

The distance of each race is given in furlongs. Steeplechase form figures are prefixed by the letter 'c' and N.H. Flat race or bumper form figures by the letter 'F', the others relating to form over hurdles.

The going is symbolised as follows: f=firm, m=good to firm, g=good, d=good to soft, dead, s=soft, v=heavy.

Placings are indicated, up to the sixth place, by use of superior figures, an asterisk being used to denote a win; and superior letters are used to convey what happened to a horse during the race: F-fell, pu-pulled up, ur-unseated rider, bd-brought down, su-slipped up, ro-ran out.

The Timeform Rating of a horse is simply the merit of the horse expressed in pounds and is arrived at by careful examination of its running against other horses. The ratings range from 175+ for the champions down to a figure of around 55 for the meanest selling platers. Symbols attached to the ratings: 'p'–likely to improve; 'P'–capable of much better form; '+' –the horse may be better than we have rated it.

An Accordion (Ire)   Timeform Rating c150p

7 b.g Accordion – Jennie's First (Idiot's Delight)
2007/8 c24m^{pu} c26d^6 c24g* c24s* Mar 11

A visor may bring out the best in Lough Derg, but in the case of the majority of David Pipe's big-race winners in 2007/8 blinkers were the headgear of choice, including for Comply Or Die in the Grand National. They certainly did the trick for An Accordion. He was fitted with blinkers for the first time when winning the Sky Bet Chase at Doncaster in January, and wore them again when showing further improvement to follow up in the William Hill Trophy at Cheltenham. A seven-year-old with just eight races outside point-

A second big handicap success for An Accordion (near side) and there's the promise of more to come

to-points under his belt, one in a bumper and seven in chases, An Accordion should go on progressing for some time yet and there are more good races to be won with him. One day he may even be capable of emulating his stablemate Comply Or Die by making his mark over the Grand National fences.

Ridden by his stable's promising conditional Johnny Farrelly at Doncaster, An Accordion gave away the initiative with sticky jumps at the final two fences before quickening back past Ungaro to win by half a length. At Cheltenham, with Tom Scudamore back on board, An Accordion again travelled strongly, and after he idled markedly after hitting the front two out, he had two and a quarter lengths to spare over nearest-pursuer New Alco at the line. A big, workmanlike gelding who typically impresses in appearance, An Accordion seems likely to stay beyond three and a quarter miles. Apart from when pulled up (reportedly distressed) on his reappearance in 2007/8, An Accordion has raced only on good ground or softer and he acts on heavy.

D E Pipe

Trainer comment: He's got to improve again this season, but he's lightly raced and blinkers have helped with his jumping.

Andytown (Ire)

5 ch.g Old Vic - Pitfire (Ire) (Parliament)
2007/8 20d 16s² 19v* 20g 24d³ Apr 23

Hexham and Catterick are unlikely to be figuring in the running plans for Andytown this season, as they were in 2007/8. The gelding, who gained his first placing over hurdles on the former course and his first win in that sphere on the latter, will be ploughing pastures new following his transfer from Nicky Richards' yard near Penrith to that of Nicky Henderson in Lambourn. Andytown didn't do himself justice on his one appearance in the South to date, finishing tailed off behind Beshabar in the EBF Final at Sandown for which he started second favourite, possibly due to the subsequent exploits of the Catterick runner-up Ignotus. Andytown was much more himself when contesting another novice handicap at Perth on his final outing of the campaign. He not only showed fairly useful form in finishing third behind The Great Alfie and My Arch there, but also shaped as if there could be still more to come, travelling strongly for a long way. Andytown's dam was a winning pointer, and he himself won a maiden point in Ireland in April 2007, shortly after which he was bought for £40,000 at the Cheltenham Sales. Clearly, the long-term future of Andytown lies over fences, but we hope his new handler will give him a few more opportunities over hurdles before then, as he looks on a potentially very favourable mark. *N J Henderson*

Trainer comment: We've schooled him over fences and he jumps well; he does everything we ask of him nicely and is very forward.

Bakbenscher

5 gr.g Bob Back (USA) – Jessolle (Scallywag)
2007/8 F16s* F16s³ F16s* Mar 31

Unlike some who have a similar title in the House of Commons, Bakbenscher does appear one to rely on from what little we have seen of him so far. The five-year-old gelding looked most genuine in his first season's racing, when making three appearances in bumpers. Bakbenscher got off the mark at the first time of asking, comfortably accounting for ten rivals in a maiden at Uttoxeter in December, and he then stepped up markedly on that form when third behind Mahonia and The Jazz Musician in a better race at Chepstow. Saving his best till last, Bakbenscher showed himself a smart bumper performer when successfully conceding weight all round in another above-average contest at Wincanton, going clear in the final furlong to win by four lengths from Aironageestring. The undoubted ability and likeable attitude he demonstrated in his first season aren't the only reasons for thinking that Bakbenscher will do very well over hurdles in his second. He also has a solid jumping pedigree—he's the first foal of the fairly useful hurdler and fair chaser Jessolle, who stayed two and a half miles—and is with a top stable, one that has a very good record with its novice hurdlers. Bakbenscher is owned by the Three Line Whip partnership, which has enjoyed great success with Blazing Bailey, a high-class hurdler who really came into his own when stepped up to two and a half miles and more. That is also likely to be the case with Bakbenscher, whose three runs to date have all been over two miles on soft ground. *A King*

Trainer comment: He's already done plenty of schooling and we'll probably start him off in novice hurdles at two miles in late-October or November; hopefully, there'll be some good races in him, as I think he's pretty high class.

Ballydub (Ire)   Timeform Rating 130p F93

5 b.g Presenting – Sovereign Leader (Ire) (Supreme Leader)
2007/8 F18v² 21s* Mar 28

Ballydub was always going to create plenty of interest when he came up for sale at Cheltenham towards the end of January. Just turned five and with a useful pedigree for jumping, the good-topped Ballydub also looked the part and had already shown a fair amount of ability, winning a maiden point in Ireland in 2007 and, on what was his only start for Henrietta Knight, finishing second in a bumper at Plumpton less than a fortnight before he appeared in the sale ring. It took a bid of £65,000 to secure him, but in the light of his one subsequent run Ballydub's connections won't be regretting a penny of it. We reckon Ballydub would fetch a good deal more if put up for sale now. Two months after joining Philip Hobbs's yard, Ballydub won a fifteen-runner maiden at Newbury on his hurdling debut, racing prominently and just getting the better of Canalturn on the run-in as the pair pulled a long way clear. It could be that Ballydub, who will stay three miles, will be let-in relatively lightly on that form, and it's to be hoped he'll be allowed to try his hand in handicap hurdles before he's switched to fences. From the family of the very smart chaser Comeragh King and the useful staying chaser Seskin Bridge, Ballydub should also be well worth following in novice chases when the time comes. *P J Hobbs*

Trainer comment: He definitely wants soft ground and a trip; he's less proven than some of ours, but I'm hopeful he'll be up to it this season.

Bene Lad (Ire)   Timeform Rating 92 c83+

6 b.g Beneficial – Sandwell Old Rose (Ire) (Roselier (Fr))
2007/8 c22m^F 25d^{pu} 21v 24v^2 c25s^{ur} 24v^3 22s* :: 2008/9 22d^2 May 6

There are plenty of better horses in this season's fifty, and also a few more able ones in Raymond Anderson-Green's ownership come to think of it, but a winner's a winner as they say and Bene Lad certainly appeals as the type to pay his way in low-grade handicaps in the North. Bene Lad has been brought along steadily by the ever-impressive Jim Goldie, and it was only in the latest season he really started to reveal his ability, confirming the promise of a couple of his earlier efforts when winning a handicap hurdle at Kelso in April in decisive fashion. A second at the same track a month later underlined his current hurdles mark isn't beyond him, particularly with further progress still a distinct possibility, but both his physique and pedigree suggest he'll be of even more interest when returned to the larger obstacles. He made two appearances over fences last season, both at Kelso, and on the second occasion was going every bit as well as the winner Dickie Lewis when hampered by that rival two out, resulting in his rider being unseated. Bene Lad, who stays three miles, has done virtually all of his racing on ground softer than good. *J S Goldie*

Trainer comment: He's been a slow-maturing horse; he's well handicapped for chasing and he's starting to get his act together.

Beshabar (Ire)   Timeform Rating 135p

6 ch.g Flemensfirth (USA) – In Our Intrest (Ire) (Buckskin (Fr))
2007/8 19s^2 19d* 19s^5 20g* Mar 8

The latest edition of Sandown's European Breeders' Fund Sunderlands 'National Hunt' Novices' Handicap Hurdle Final was won in decisive fashion by the least experienced of the seventeen who contested it. Beshabar, a six-year-old with only three races under his belt, began to get on top between the last two flights and ran on strongly up the hill to pull three and three quarter lengths clear, adding to the win he'd gained in a novice event at Exeter a little more than five weeks earlier. There is no doubt that Beshabar would have a bright future kept to hurdling, but like many in what was a good-looking field at Sandown he has the build of one who will make an even better chaser. The 2007 Final was won by Albertas Run, who twelve months later was successful in the Royal & SunAlliance Chase at Cheltenham, and it certainly isn't out of the question that the big, well-made Beshabar, who raced off a mark 7 lb higher than Albertas Run had done, could emulate him. If he does it won't be for Nick Williams' small stable, one which continues to punch above its weight and remains well worth following. Beshabar, having been sold in a private deal to Denman's part-owner Harry Findlay, will be in training with Paul Nicholls this season.

Given the manner in which he finished his race at Sandown, Beshabar should have no trouble staying three miles, a view supported by his pedigree. Beshabar's sire Flemensfirth is responsible for plenty who stay that far, while there is an abundance of stamina in the bottom half of the pedigree. With the potential to win races at the highest level when sent over fences, Beshabar is an exciting prospect and very much one to follow. *P F Nicholls*

Trainer comment: He's a decent addition to the string, and I'm looking forward to him going novice chasing.

Bible Lord (Ire)

Timeform Rating c140

7 ch.g Mister Lord (USA) – Pharisee (Ire) (Phardante (Fr))
2007/8 c24d⁴ c26v c24d⁶ c19s* c20d⁴ c25d Apr 4

That Bible Lord won only once last season doesn't represent anything like a fair reflection of his progress, and this imposing chaser can surely make amends for his lack of success this time around. Lack of stamina found Bible Lord out on three of his starts in 2007/8, whilst jumping errors held him back on other occasions, including when Bible Lord posted highly encouraging efforts in both the Racing Post Plate at Cheltenham and another valuable event at Aintree on his last two appearances. Bible Lord made several mistakes in the former, so it says plenty for his ability that he finished so strongly to take fourth, with subsequent Topham Chase winner Gwanako and

the well-handicapped veteran Mister McGoldrick two of those ahead of him. Aintree was a similar story, as a combination of errors over demanding fences and a return to further than three miles led to Bible Lord weakening out of things in the straight having again travelled strongly. Don't be fooled into thinking Bible Lord's credentials for this season are built solely on the hope his jumping improves, though; after all, he's only 7 lb higher than when drawing a distance clear with The Sawyer at Exeter in February, the one time everything clicked with him. In addition, connections have so far remained loyal to Mark Grant (who's ridden the gelding on all ten chase starts) but it wouldn't be the biggest surprise if a higher-profile jockey replaced him at some stage. Valuable handicaps beckon for Bible Lord again this season, so plenty of pressure will once more be placed upon his fencing, but if it goes as smoothly as is hoped he'll be a major force in a good number of them.
Andrew Turnell

Trainer comment: He's ahead of schedule and I think we'll start him off around two and a half miles—the Paddy Power is his main early-season aim.

Big Fella Thanks

Timeform Rating 135p

6 b.g Primitive Rising (USA) – Nunsdream (Derrylin)
2007/8 24v* 24s* 24d² Apr 18

The two horses who fought out the finish of division one of the five-year-old geldings maiden point at Carrigtwohill on February 4th 2007 ended up in the same ownership and went on to win a couple of races each over hurdles for Paul Nicholls in 2007/8. Big Fella Thanks, who edged out Herecomesthetruth in that point, also proved the better of the pair over hurdles, showing useful form, and he very much appeals as the sort to do well over fences this season. He's certainly bred for chasing, and also for stamina. By Primitive Rising, his unraced dam is out of a half-sister to the 1992 Eider Chase winner David's Duky and the good hunter chaser Rolls Rambler. Big Fella Thanks has looked a thorough stayer in his three starts to date over hurdles, all of them taking place over three miles on ground softer than good. He won the first two, beating the fairly useful Buck The Legend by ten lengths in a maiden at Chepstow in January and landing the odds by nine lengths at Taunton later the same month. Given a short break, Big Fella Thanks returned to show even better form in defeat. Carrying top weight in a novice handicap at Ayr, Big Fella Thanks gave best only after the last in finishing runner-up to the much improved Asian Royale (rec 11 lb), who had won handicaps at Navan and Fairyhouse on his previous two starts. Brought along quietly so far, Big Fella Thanks is now all set to make a name for himself as a staying novice chaser. *P F Nicholls*

Trainer comment: He's huge; he took well to hurdles and will do even better over fences over long distances.

Blackpool Billy (Ire) — Timeform Rating 111 F103

6 br.g Overbury (Ire) – Ina's Farewell (Random Shot)
2007/8 F16s* F16s³ 19d⁶ 16v* 16v* 20d² Mar 22

Trevor Hemmings, who cemented his position amongst the top National Hunt owners in Britain last season, is probably better known in the wider world through his ownership of Blackpool Tower. Therefore, sentiment might well have been a factor in Hemmings' private purchase of Blackpool Billy prior to the six-year-old's hurdling debut in January. Whatever the reasoning behind the deal, though, it looks yet another shrewd buy on Hemmings' part given the impression the gelding made in 2007/8. Blackpool Billy was owned by his trainer Ferdy Murphy when giving the first sign of his potential in bumpers, running out a 20/1-winner at Towcester in November before emerging as the best at the weights under a penalty at Haydock the following month. Yet, judged on pedigree, it was as a jumper that Blackpool Billy was always likely to shine, and Hemmings received a quick return on his investment when Blackpool Billy took a maiden at Ayr on just his second start over hurdles. After following up at Hexham, Blackpool Billy made a most encouraging handicap debut at Haydock, where he found only the progressive and more experienced Hopkins (also owned by Hemmings) too good. Connections have expressed a wish to send Blackpool Billy chasing, but it's to be hoped they give him the opportunity to take full advantage of a lenient handicap mark over hurdles before then. *Ferdy Murphy*

Trainer comment: He's done quite a bit of cantering already and will probably go novice chasing; I think he can take the next step forward, and he could be a SunAlliance horse.

Carrickmines (Ire)   Timeform Rating 95

6 b.g Saddlers' Hall (Ire) – Orla's Castle (Ire) (Bulldozer)
2007/8 F16s F16g⁴ 22m⁴ 16g 17g 16s 20s⁶ 17s⁴ 21g :: 2008/9 20d⁵ 24g⁶ May 16

Carrickmines is still a maiden after twelve starts and has shown modest form at best over hurdles in the last nine of them, but he has displayed more than enough promise to suggest that it is only a matter of time before he scores his first success. And a change of stable certainly won't have harmed his prospects, given the declining fortunes of his previous handler Steve Brookshaw, who hit the heights with Grand National winner Lord Gyllene in 1997 but has had only fourteen winners under both codes since Cassia Heights took the 2004 Topham. Bought for £30,000 at the Doncaster May Sales, Carrickmines is now with Dr. Richard Newland who has enjoyed great success with seemingly exposed jumpers he has purchased from other yards, notably Burntoakboy and Overstrand. Carrickmines put up his best performance over hurdles on his final start for Brookshaw, finishing sixth of seventeen when stepped up to three miles in a novice handicap at Aintree early on in the current season. A BHA mark of 92 underestimates his ability, and in the belief that Dr. Newland can get the best out of him we think Carrickmines will be well worth following in handicap hurdles. A big, lengthy, good sort, he will also be of interest when he goes over fences.
Dr R D P Newland

Trainer comment: We've just done a wind op on him which should be a positive and he'll be ready to run around Christmas; he's got the size and scope of a good horse, and he's got to be well handicapped.

Conflictofinterest   Timeform Rating F110p

6 b.g Saddlers' Hall (Ire) – Fortune's Girl (Ardross)
2007/8 F16g² F16g* Apr 19

A strong individual with a good jumping pedigree and from a top yard, and who has shown himself more than useful in a couple of starts in bumpers, Conflictofinterest has plenty going for him as he embarks on his career over jumps. Well supported on his debut, at Ascot in February, Conflictofinterest shaped well in finishing two lengths second to previous winner Gold Award, his inexperience just counting against him in the closing stages. Two months later Conflictofinterest impressed when going one better at Ayr, in a race where all bar one of those who had run before had won or been placed. Conflictofinterest was soon in front and hardly had to be asked a question in order to draw clear of his rivals in the straight, still showing signs of greenness but having plenty of running left in him at the finish. His nearest pursuer Knockara Beau, who was six lengths adrift, was to give the form a boost when winning at Aintree in May. Conflictofinterest is closely related to the useful hurdler Theatre Girl (by King's Theatre) and a half-brother to the smart hurdler Ring The Boss (by Kahyasi) and fairly useful hurdler Diamond Sal (by Bob Back), all of whom stay two and a half miles. Their dam Fortune's Girl was a winning hurdler/chaser who stayed twenty-seven furlongs. Likely to stay at least two and a half miles himself, Conflictofinterest looks an exciting prospect for novice hurdles this season. *P F Nicholls*

Trainer comment: He was impressive at Ayr and is ready to do his job over hurdles.

Cornas (NZ)

Timeform Rating 119p

6 br.g Prized (USA) – Duvessa (NZ) (Sound Reason (Can)) 2007/8 F16d F16d⁶ 17g⁵ 16s⁵ 16g* :: 2008/9 16g² May 24

There aren't many better stables to follow than that of Nick Williams, who increased his previous best total of winners in a season by one in 2007/8 and continues to place his horses very astutely—anyone shrewd enough to put £1 on every one of his runners in the last three seasons would have shown a profit of almost £100. Williams will have to make do in 2008/9 without useful novice hurdler Beshabar, who was sold privately to join Paul Nicholls after his Sandown win, but he has much to look forward to as far as Diamond Harry is concerned, while Cornas is another who looks sure to win more races for him.

Following two runs in bumpers for Evan Williams, Cornas was switched to hurdles upon joining his present yard and on his third start over them improved considerably to upset the odds laid on Albinus in a novice at Wincanton, beating him by one and a half lengths with a further fifteen lengths back to the third. Cornas ran every bit as well on his only outing since, in a handicap at Stratford early on in the current season, taking second behind the impressive Woolcombe Folly despite things not going his way.

That proved strong form, with all bar one of the six from the first eight to have run since winning next time out, and it's most unlikely we have seen the best of Cornas yet. Connections have the option of running him back in a novice before the end of October, and the likelihood is he'd be up to defying a penalty in such company. *Nick Williams*

Trainer comment: He's got scope and I think there's a decent two-mile handicap in him—I see him as a totesport Trophy type of horse.

Diamond Harry

Timeform Rating F116

**5 b.g Sir Harry Lewis (USA) – Swift Conveyance (Ire) (Strong Gale)
2007/8 F16s* Mar 29**

As doubles go, the one completed by Diamond Harry at Newbury in March has to go down as one of the most unusual, his victory in the very valuable DBS Spring Sales Bumper coming on only his second start and just over twelve months after he'd made a successful debut in the same contest. It was not only a notable feat of training, but also of race-planning. Diamond Harry's connections took the view that it was worth putting him aside for a second crack at the big prize while he was still eligible (the race is open only to four- and five-year-olds), a potentially more rewarding ploy than a season in novice hurdles which could, in any event, be delayed for a year.

In 2007 Diamond Harry had been a 33/1-shot when coming from off the pace to win by half a length. A year on he shared favouritism with the Kempton winner Riverside Theatre and the most expensive runner in the line-up Bobby On The Beat, a debutant from the Paul Nicholls stable. As had been the case the previous year, conditions were testing and Diamond Harry was one of the few to cope, making the running on this occasion and finding plenty when challenged. He held on only by a short head from the Wincanton winner Shalone, but the pair were eight lengths clear of Riverside Theatre who was in turn more than twenty lengths clear of the remainder. It was a smart performance from Diamond Harry, a fair step up on his 2007 effort, Shalone franking the form when winning impressively at Uttoxeter in May. Diamond Harry, whose dam was a modest winner over hurdles, best at around two miles, is now all set to begin his hurdling career. The next five horses who followed him in the 2007 Newbury race all went on to win over hurdles in the next season, and the rangy Diamond Harry looks sure to do well himself in novice events. *Nick Williams*

Trainer comment: He's scheduled to follow the same path as Beshabar and will start in an EBF qualifier at Uttoxeter in October.

Forest Pennant (Ire)   Timeform Rating 137p

6 b.g Accordion – Prudent View (Ire) (Supreme Leader)
2007/8 20d² 19s³ 20v* 19d* 20g⁴ 24g* Apr 5

Much is known about Paul Nicholls' team of novice hurdlers from 2007/8, especially those who featured in the major events at Cheltenham. Forest Pennant had a much lower profile than the likes of Celestial Halo, The Tother One and Rippling Ring for most of last season, but given the form he showed in handicaps on his last two starts there is every reason to believe he can progress as far as any of those mentioned, especially once switching to fences. After winning novice events at Chepstow and Taunton in February, Forest Pennant showed much improved form in defeat on his handicap debut, in the EBF Final at Sandown, finishing fourth behind his now-stablemate Beshabar. Stepped up to three miles and able to run from the same BHA mark, Forest Pennant justified favouritism in a twenty-two runner listed handicap at Aintree on Grand National day, staying on strongly after being left with plenty to do to beat the progressive Superior Wisdom by a length and a quarter, the pair finishing clear. While he is certainly capable of winning more races over hurdles, it's more than likely that Forest Pennant will have his attentions turned to chasing sooner rather than later, and he looks the type to do even better in that sphere. Forest Pennant, who will stay beyond three miles, has raced on good ground or softer and acts on heavy. *P F Nicholls*

Trainer comment: He did very well over hurdles and is now ready for novice chasing.

Gee Dee Nen   Timeform Rating 84p

5 b.g Mister Baileys – Special Beat (Bustino)
2007/8 NR :: 2008/9 NR (Aug9F*)

Gee Dee Nen's hurdling career was put on hold after just one run, in a juvenile event at Market Rasen in March 2007, but it's due to resume this season and we fully expect him to leave the form he showed that day well behind when he does return. Gee Dee Nen looked in need of a greater test of stamina when sixth to River Logic over an extended seventeen furlongs at Market Rasen, keeping on from three out to be nearest at the finish, and his performances on the Flat since support that view. Although pretty useful at up to a mile and three quarters on the Flat at the time of his hurdling debut, Gee Dee Nen has proved even better campaigned mainly at two miles since. In 2008 he has been successful over the trip at both Haydock and Ascot, on the latter course staying on strongly to lead close home in the Shergar Cup Stayers, a truly-run contest which took place in quite testing conditions. Following that victory Gee Dee Nen was sold privately and left Mark Tompkins for Jim Best, a trainer who features in the 'Future Stars' section of this publication and who can be guaranteed to exploit the gelding's hurdling potential to the full. Gee Dee Nen, who will really come into his own over two and a half miles and more, has shown his form on the Flat on ground ranging from soft to good to firm. *Jim Best*

Trainer comment: He won on Shergar Cup day and had some other solid form to his name on the Flat; he's still in the Cesarewitch, so we'll probably go for that before sending him back hurdling.

General Potter

Timeform Rating 88p F-

6 b.g Overbury (Ire) – Potter's Gale (Ire) (Strong Gale)
2007/8 F16v⁶ 19s 20s⁶ 20d⁴ Apr 25

General Potter wasn't among those who helped make the 2007/8 season such a successful one for the Donald McCain stable, but we fully expect him to play his part in 2008/9. Brought along very steadily so far—his debut came in a bumper in February—the six-year-old didn't do much more than potter round on his first three starts, but he shaped with much more promise on his fourth. In a twelve-runner maiden hurdle at Bangor won by the useful Canalturn, who started odds on, 33/1-shot General Potter raced prominently for a long way before fading into fourth, still showing signs of inexperience. There's almost certainly a fair bit more to come from General Potter, and he'll be of more interest now he's been allotted a handicap mark. Pedigree-wise, General Potter, who is likely to stay beyond two and a half miles, has plenty to live up to. His dam Potter's Gale, a useful hurdler and fairly useful chaser, is a half-sister to Denman, and she has already produced three winners. They include General Potter's year-older full-sister Missis Potts, who developed into a useful hurdler in 2007/8 and also created a good impression when successful on her chasing debut. *D McCain Jnr*

Trainer comment: He's had his problems, but he's a big horse and seemed to be getting the hang of things late on; he'll go novice handicap chasing sooner rather than later.

Gwanako (Fr)

Timeform Rating 147 c148p

5 b.g Sin Kiang (Fr) – Vaubecourt (Fr) (Courtroom (Fr))
2007/8 16d* 16d³ 21g⁴ 16d⁵ c20d³ c20d² c21d* Apr 4

Undoubtedly smart but seemingly with his limitations exposed over hurdles, Gwanako was sent chasing after the turn of the year, although he wasn't qualified for novice events as he had won on his only outing over fences in France as a three-year-old. Remarkably, it took him just three runs to reach the level he had as a hurdler, and we have no doubt that there is still better to come from Gwanako the chaser.

Let down by his jumping when beaten at odds on in his first start over fences in Britain, Gwanako proved considerably more fluent and left that form well behind in the Racing Post Plate at Cheltenham, pulling well clear of the remainder as he gave chase to the runaway winner Mister McGoldrick.

Gwanako makes light of jumping one of Aintree's big fences en route to success in the Topham

Another strongly-contested handicap, the John Smith's Topham Chase, promised to provide a still more searching examination of Gwanako's jumping and of his general lack of experience, given that it's run over Aintree's National fences and had twenty-nine participants. In the event, Gwanako proved more than up to the task. Jumping fluently apart from at the water, Gwanako was soon travelling strongly in touch in a well-run race which took its toll on the field (only a dozen completed) and, after quickening to lead at the last, held on by a neck from Irish Raptor. His performance encouraged speculation about his Grand National prospects, but stamina is a problem where that race is concerned—Gwanako probably wouldn't have lasted home even in the Topham if it had still been run over the full two miles and six furlongs. There should be plenty of opportunities for Gwanako to enhance his record over fences in 2008/9, with return visits to Cheltenham and Aintree presumably on the cards. Gwanako, a small, strong gelding, has raced only on good ground or softer. *P F Nicholls*

Trainer comment: He took well to the fences at Aintree and will head back there for a very valuable race in the autumn.

Island Flyer (Ire)   Timeform Rating 93 c124p

6 b.g Heron Island (Ire) – Lindas Statement (Ire) (Strong Statement (USA))
2007/8 21s^{pu} 16d^4 16s^6 22g c18d* c21d* c22s* Mar 28

Island Flyer hardly set the world alight in four starts over hurdles, but he's been on fire since switched to fences. A tall half-brother to a couple of winning pointers, Island Flyer had won such an event in Ireland himself and it was on the cards that he would prove more effective as a chaser. Even so, his progress has been remarkable, unbeaten in three starts in the space of a month. The feature of his successes has been his bold jumping from the front, looking very accomplished for a novice, while he's also shown versatility so far as trip is concerned. His first win (at Newbury) came over two and a quarter miles, while he completed the hat-trick (at the same coure) over two and three quarter miles in a race that largely worked out well, shaping as if three miles will be well within his range in scoring by a length from Appleaday. Though undoubtedly well treated under a penalty, Island Flyer remained on the bridle for much longer than most of his rivals that day and the winning margin undersold his superiority somewhat, so there's every

Another bold-jumping front-running display from Island Flyer

reason to think that Island Flyer hasn't finished progressing. He's raced only on good ground or softer so far. **T R George**

Trainer comment: He's matured and strengthened up since last season; he's a staying chaser and there's a valuable race at Wincanton he could go for early on.

Knockara Beau (Ire)   Timeform Rating F107

5 b.g Leading Counsel (USA) – Clairabell (Ire) (Buckskin (Fr))
2007/8 F16v* F16g² :: 2008/9 F17g* May 16

Considering that Knockara Beau is bred to be suited by long distances, the fact he showed a useful level of form whilst winning two of his three starts in bumpers is particularly encouraging, and it'll be surprising if plenty more success doesn't come his way in novice hurdles in the coming months. Indeed, the only horse to beat Knockara Beau to date is the very exciting Conflictofinterest, and the chances are he won't come up against many of his calibre this season if, as expected, he's campaigned mainly in the North. It wasn't as if Knockara Beau needed testing conditions to show his form in bumpers, either, even if his debut win at Kelso came on heavy going. The ground was nothing like as soft when he chased home Conflictofinterest at Ayr or when he typically battled on gamely to hold off Son of Flicka and Karabak at Aintree in May. George Charlton had already trained more winners in 2008 by the end of March than he did in all of his first year in charge of his family's yard, and Knockara Beau for one should help ensure the scoreboard keeps ticking over. *G A Charlton*

Trainer comment: He'll go hurdling now and we'll win one or two with him and see where we go from there—he's real quality; he'll probably want two and a half miles plus.

Mad Max (Ire)   Timeform Rating F120

6 b.g Kayf Tara – Carole's Crusader (Faustus (USA))
2007/8 F16s* F16d* Feb 9

That he should be so well backed on his debut, when up against course-and-distance winner The Big Orse and twelve others in a bumper at Newbury, suggested that Mad Max had been showing star quality at home, and the six-

There's no catching the enormous Mad Max

year-old readily justified the support. Yet it was his performance when following up on his return to the course fifteen days later that really put Mad Max in the spotlight. In a Grade 2 contest generally regarded as one of the strongest bumpers run prior to the Cheltenham Festival, one won in recent times by the likes of Iris's Gift and Cornish Rebel, Mad Max smashed up a field which included five other previous winners, leading a furlong out and winning going away by eight lengths from The Nightingale. Only dual Grade 1 winner Cousin Vinny showed markedly better form in bumpers in the 2007/8 campaign, and Mad Max already looks a potential A-lister.

Just about the most encouraging element of Mad Max's bumper achievements was that he showed sufficient speed to run to such a high level despite his pedigree—by the dual Ascot Gold Cup winner Kayf Tara out of Carole's Crusader, who was a thorough stayer over fences, albeit one with a fair bit of ability as well. Mad Max will be suited by two and a half miles plus, and with his imposing physique he looks sure to make a major impact in novice events in the coming months. *N J Henderson*

Trainer comment: They don't come any bigger than him, he's gigantic; he's schooled over hurdles and, whilst they might get in the way of him, I'm not keen on sending them straight from bumpers to fences.

Metaphoric (Ire)   Timeform Rating 123+

4 b.g Montjeu (Ire) – Virgin Hawk (USA) (Silver Hawk (USA)) 2007/8 16g² 16s⁴ 16g* 16s⁵ 17g* Apr 6 :: 2008/9 NR (Jul12F*)

The surface has barely been scratched where Metaphoric's potential as a hurdler is concerned. Two wins from five outings in juvenile events isn't a bad start but, from what we know of him on the Flat, there is surely a good deal better to come when he's given the opportunity to tackle two and a half miles and more, while his jumping should become more fluent as he gains further experience. The aforementioned wins came at Warwick and Market Rasen, and Metaphoric also acquitted himself quite well in a much more competitive event in between, when fifth to Crack Away Jack in the listed Fred Winter Handicap at the Cheltenham Festival after being involved in scrimmaging at the second and left with a lot to do after being hampered again approaching three out. Since his last run over hurdles Metaphoric has had two outings on the Flat at Ascot, running respectably when third over two miles six furlongs in the Queen Alexandra Stakes at the Royal meeting then showing smart form when winning a two-mile handicap. He was visored on the latter occasion, and it is possible that headgear will also benefit him when he returns to hurdling. *M L W Bell*

Trainer comment: He'll definitely be campaigned over hurdles in staying handicaps; he's a far more mature horse and has filled out now.

Mous of Men (Fr)

Timeform Rating 131

5 b.g Lord of Men – Mousmee (Fr) (Kaldounevees (Fr))
2007/8 19m⁴ 18s² 16s* 19g* 16d 17g 19m* Apr 26

The victories of Comply Or Die in the Grand National and Our Vic in the Ryanair Chase and totesport Bowl were the highlights of the 2007/8 season for David Pipe. He also achieved another notable landmark at a much lower level when progressive young hurdler Mous of Men, on just his second outing after leaving Henrietta Knight, gave his stable its one hundredth winner of the campaign, at Sandown on the final day of the season. Mous of Men had shown fairly useful form and won two races for Knight, the second of those a handicap at Doncaster run over a distance just short of two and a half miles, and it was a return to that trip at Sandown, following a couple of defeats around two miles, that saw Mous of Men record comfortably his best effort. In what was another competitive-looking handicap, Mous of Men won by three lengths from Mexican Pete, shaping as though he will probably stay a bit further. Mous of Men, who impressed with his jumping at Sandown, may have even more to offer over hurdles, but it's for his potential as a chaser that he's been included here. Mous of Men, who wears a tongue strap, is a chasing type in appearance and is with a stable which does well with its novice chasers, so he can hardly fail to win races when he goes over fences. He has won on ground ranging from soft to good to firm. *D E Pipe*

Trainer comment: He'll probably go novice chasing; he's still young and hopefully can improve.

Mr Strachan (Ire)

7 b.g Zaffaran (USA) – Call Girl (Ire) (Dromod Hill)
2007/8 c20d² c20d² c22s² c20d* c24d³ c20dᶠ c25d c25g³ Apr 19

The eleven-year-old Mister McGoldrick was still doing the Sue Smith stable proud last season, showing himself better than ever when winning the Racing Post Plate at Cheltenham. However, he can only go on for so long and his trainer will be looking to some of his much younger stablemates to come through the ranks and make a similar impact in good-class chases. Mr Strachan may well be one who proves up to the task. A fairly useful performer over hurdles who always looked the sort to make an even better chaser, Mr Strachan duly proved as much in his first season over fences in 2007/8 and seems sure to go on and do well in open company. Mr Strachan was also in action at the Cheltenham Festival but not for very long, a fifth-fence faller in the Jewson Novices' Handicap for which he started favourite. That was the only occasion Mr Strachan failed to complete in eight starts over fences. He generally jumped soundly, including when beating the subsequent Arkle runner-up Kruguyrova by two and a half lengths at Wetherby in December,

Mr Strachan is unexposed so far as staying handicap chases are concerned

racing prominently as he often does. The consistent Mr Strachan will stay beyond twenty-five furlongs; he acts on heavy going and is untested on firmer than good. *Mrs S J Smith*

Trainer comment: We will be looking at longer distances and handicaps, though he will probably start off in an intermediate event at Carlisle.

Osana (Fr)

Timeform Rating 162

6 b.g Video Rock (Fr) – Voilette (Fr) (Brezzo (Fr)
2007/8 16s² 17g* 16s² 20g² Apr 5

Nominated as an Arkle candidate last autumn, when he made plenty of appeal as a novice chaser, Osana was kept to hurdling and developed into one of the best around. Yet Osana still has the potential to be an even better chaser than hurdler, and hopefully he will get the opportunity to prove as much sooner rather than later, though that's not to say he won't still be worth following if he continues over hurdles. Osana made four appearances over hurdles in 2007/8, the first three at Cheltenham. A good second under top weight to Sizing Europe in the Greatwood Hurdle was followed by a victory in the boylesports.com International Hurdle, Osana taking a six-length lead from the gate, maintaining a good gallop all the way and winning by eight lengths from Katchit. Osana had clearly arrived as a candidate for top honours, as usual impressing with his fluent jumping, and even though unable to confirm placings with Katchit in the Champion Hurdle he emerged with his reputation enhanced. Not only did Osana maintain a strong pace on more testing ground but he also showed plenty of resolution once headed two out, going down by only a length. It is likely that Osana wasn't fully over that hard race when second again, below form this time, to Al Eile in the Aintree Hurdle. That was Osana's second start at two and a half miles and he has yet to show his form over the trip, though he should stay at least that far on pedigree. Osana, unraced on anything firmer than good, acts well on soft going. *D E Pipe*

Trainer comment: He'll be hurdling again this season and will probably start in the International; he's lightly raced and hopefully open to a bit more improvement.

Oscar Gogo (Ire)

6 b.g Oscar (Ire) – Ceolbridgequeen (Ire) (Executive Perk)
2007/8 F16m* F16v[4] 19v[5] 16s[3] 20m :: 2008/9 20d[4] 16s[4] Sep 14

There already looked to be plenty of positives about Oscar Gogo's prospects for the season before his eye-catching return at Stratford, and there's even less doubt now he can be placed to advantage in handicap hurdles in 2008/9. Oscar Gogo was an above-average bumper winner early last season, so he could have been viewed as disappointing in his first four runs over hurdles, but he went as if all his ability was intact when placed behind the subsequently-disqualified Ignotus at Newcastle on his second try, and he left the impression at Stratford he will prove a better horse for a change of stable, having left Howard Johnson since last seen in the spring. He's started life in handicap hurdles on a potentially lenient mark given his bumper form, and has looked a stayer, so it was a little surprising to see him ridden patiently at Stratford considering he was dropped to two miles, and less surprising he was doing all his best work at the finish. Add to that the fact he wasn't knocked about, either, and everything looks in place for the six-year-old belatedly to start fulfilling his initial promise, particularly when returned to further.
L Corcoran

Trainer comment: The plan is to try and win a race with him; he's been pleasing us and he jumps well.

Pasco (Swi)

5 gr.g Selkirk (USA) – Palena (Danehill (USA))
2007/8 16s[2] 16s* 16d* 16s[pu] Mar 11

The unraced Palena has more than made up for her lack of racing miles with a far from sedentary stud career. Her first foal, the unraced Biquette, was conceived in France, born in Britain and by the New Zealand-bred, Australian champion Octagonal. Next came Pasco, who was conceived in Britain and born in Switzerland. Since Pasco, Palena has had a filly by the then Swiss-based Arazi, foaling this time in Ireland, before visiting Italy for a liaison with King Charlemagne, producing a filly once returned to Switzerland.

Pasco is himself already a fairly seasoned traveller, sent from his country of birth to race for trainer Henri-Alex Pantall in France. Pasco made his debut as a three-year-old, winning a newcomers event at Nantes, setting up a solid if unspectacular career on the level, winning once more from a further ten starts. After his final outing in France, Pasco was bought privately by Terry Warner as a jumping prospect. His first three outings over hurdles were all at Newbury, where after initially being beaten into second by Helen's Vision he comfortably won a maiden and a novice, beating Lupanar by six lengths in the latter. Pasco was then pitched in at the deep end in an open-looking Supreme Novices' Hurdle, and whilst he disappointed there and has a Flat pedigree, he still appeals as the type to take high rank amongst the novice chasers in 2008/9—like many by his sire he has plenty of size. He should stay beyond two miles, though the way he has travelled through his races shows he's not short of speed. *P F Nicholls*

Trainer comment: He was possibly over the top at Cheltenham and the break has done him the world of good.

Pettifour (Ire)

Timeform Rating 146p F101

6 b.g Supreme Leader – Queen of Natives (Ire) (Be My Native (USA)
2007/8 F16d^4 F16s^2 20v* 21d* 24d* Apr 4

Pettifour's victory in the Grade 1 Sefton Novices' Hurdle at Aintree in April was a second in the race for trainer Nigel Twiston-Davies and came nine years after his first, with King's Road. In many ways Pettifour resembles King's Road, who went on to show very smart form over fences, including when winning the 2000 Hennessy at Newbury. Yet at the moment Twiston-Davies is unsure whether the six-year-old will be going chasing in 2008/9 or be aimed at the World Hurdle. We are hoping it will be the former. While he might make the progress required to threaten Inglis Drever, Kasbah Bliss, Blazing Bailey and the like, Pettifour's physique, demeanour and pedigree all shout steeplechasing.

Pettifour won both his starts over hurdles prior to Aintree, in novice company at Hereford and Newbury, by a length and a quarter at the latter from another who features among the fifty, The Jazz Musician. The step up to three miles in the Sefton looked sure to show Pettifour in an even better light, and so it turned out. Up against several who already had smart performances to their name at graded level, 16/1-shot Pettifour proved more than their equal, cutting out some of the early running, responding really well to regain the lead at the last and holding on by a neck from Gone To Lunch, the pair

Pettifour (yellow armbands) takes his unbeaten record over hurdles to three despite a marked step up in class

pulling five lengths and more clear of the remainder. The strong, useful-looking Pettifour, who will stay beyond three miles, has raced on going softer than good and he acts on heavy. *N A Twiston-Davies*

Trainer comment: His aim is the West Yorkshire Hurdle at Wetherby and if he doesn't win or go close in that he'll go novice chasing.

Planet of Sound   Timeform Rating 131

6 b.g Kayf Tara – Herald The Dawn (Dubassoff (USA))
2007/8 16d* 17s² 16s⁴ 16d² 16d² 16g* Apr 12

Owner-breeder Charles Lloyd-Baker has had little reason to regret hanging on to the final three foals produced by his prolific broodmare Herald The Dawn prior to her death in 2004. From Dawn To Dusk has carried Lloyd-Baker's purple and white colours to victory no less than seven times, whilst his three-years-younger half-brother Planet of Sound could well better that tally over the next few years. He marked himself out as a good prospect on his hurdling debut when winning a maiden event at Chepstow by four lengths from The Package, and developed into a useful novice as the season progressed, putting up his best performance on his penultimate start in a handicap at Haydock, where he finished one and a quarter lengths second to Doctor David, who benefited from a good tactical ride, the pair pulling well clear of the remainder. Planet of Sound rounded off his campaign with a workmanlike success back in novice company at Newbury where he dictated the pace and beat Calgary Bay by two lengths. Set to start the new campaign off a BHA mark of 132, Planet of Sound will be one to note in handicap hurdles if he steps up to around two and a half miles, a trip which has looked certain to suit more than once. Should he be switched to fences Planet of Sound would be of even more interest as he's a tall gelding, more a chaser than hurdler on looks. *P J Hobbs*

Trainer comment: He's definitely going novice chasing; it will be two miles to start with, but he'll want two and a half and I hope there's plenty of time for him to get better.

Pterodactyl (Ire)

Timeform Rating 111p

6 b.g Montjeu (Ire) – Blue Kestrel (Ire) (Bluebird (USA))
2007/8 17s² 20s⁴ 16g² Apr 10

Pterodactyl hasn't landed in the winner's enclosure on a British racecourse as yet, but it surely won't be long before he does. A fairly useful performer on the Flat in France, when trained by John Hammond, Pterodactyl finished in the frame on all three starts for current connections in his first season over hurdles, looking unlucky when runner-up in two-mile novice events at Taunton and Towcester. A mistake at the last proved costly on the former course, while he was left with too much to do when beaten a length and three quarters by previous winner Pop on the latter, running on really strongly from two out when finally asked for greater effort. He left the strong impression he should have run out an emphatic winner that day, and it came as no surprise when his jockey Liam Treadwell was handed a ten-day ban for riding an ill-judged race. In between those runs, Pterodactyl seemed to find his stamina stretched over two and a half miles on soft ground at Chepstow, and while he may stay that far under less testing conditions it could be that he will prove best around two miles. Pterodactyl had form over as far as a mile and a half on the Flat but his two wins in that sphere came at shorter, the second of them in a mile-and-a-quarter handicap at Longchamp in September in which he wore blinkers. Incidentally, both wins were gained on good to firm going, although he also proved effective on soft. *Miss Venetia Williams*

Trainer comment: He's still a novice so we'll stick to those races initially and, although he ended up looking a stayer at Towcester, we'll play it by ear with regards the trip, depending on the ground.

Punchestowns (Fr)   Timeform Rating 135

5 ch.g Morespeed – History (Fr) (Alesso (USA))
2007/8 16g* 20s* 21g³ Apr 18

It seems that every season Nicky Henderson unleashes a number of promising hurdlers that come to him from off the Flat in France, the Supreme Novices' runner-up and Aintree winner Binocular the pick of the arrivals in 2007/8. Following his arrival from Phillipe Chemin's stable, Punchestowns didn't go on to achieve as much as Binocular in his first season in Britain, steered away from the Festival meetings, but in winning two of his three starts he created a very good impression and looks one to follow. Punchestowns' two-length debut win, at Sandown, was followed by a facile success in another novice at Uttoxeter. He showed useful form at the latter course and matched it when beaten in a stronger contest at Cheltenham. There he shaped as if he's capable

There are more races to be won with the promising Punchestowns

of better still in finishing thirteen lengths third to Elusive Dream, his jumping not so polished as some of his rivals after just the two runs, which took its toll on the uphill finish. In the longer term, the well-made Punchestowns looks very much the sort to do well over fences. *N J Henderson*

Trainer comment: I think we might keep him over hurdles for the time being; he was green last season and is promising.

Putney Bridge   Timeform Rating F105p

6 b.g Slip Anchor – Mayroni (Bustino)
2007/8 F16g* F19g⁴ F16s* Mar 29

Former Welsh champion point-to-point rider Tim Vaughan has started to make a name for himself as a trainer in recent months, boasting an impressive strike rate whilst sending out over twenty winners between May and August, and he made another significant career move when agreeing to take over the running of owner Dai Walters' yard, previously the responsibility of Helen Lewis. Miss Lewis sent out thirteen winners over the course of the last two seasons, among them the fairly useful hurdlers Helens Vision and National Trust, and also enjoyed some success in bumpers, Lord Generous landing a listed event at Cheltenham last winter. Her penultimate victory came via Putney Bridge, who was winning for a third time when making all in ready fashion at Stratford in March. Putney Bridge had previously landed a point-to-point and another bumper when trained in Ireland and, whilst both the bumper races he won lacked strength in depth, the horse he beat at Stratford, No Panic, has made up into a fairly useful hurdler. Putney Bridge is likely to stay a fair bit further than his brother, the fair two-mile hurdler Caulkleys Bank; he has the scope to make an impression himself over jumps and should help bring his young trainer even more to the racing public's attention. *Tim Vaughan*

Trainer comment: He'll go novice hurdling; he shows us plenty at home and the form of his bumper win in the spring has worked out well with No Panic finishing second over hurdles at Galway at the end of July.

Quaddick Lake (Ire)

Timeform Rating 113

5 br.g Blueprint (Ire) – Wondermac (Ire) (Jeu de Paille (Fr))
2007/8 16g^F 16g 16s Jan 25

Quaddick Lake's profile is similar to the one Bannow Strand, also owned by David Johnson, had at the same stage of his career. Both won a maiden point in Ireland as a four-year-old and showed promise in a light first season over hurdles while giving the impression they wouldn't really come into their own until tackling fences. We nominated Bannow Strand as one to follow in 2005/6 and he won a couple of chases, showing useful form, and now we are looking to Quaddick Lake to pay his way in his second season, be it over hurdles or fences. Quaddick Lake needs to put a couple of disappointing efforts behind him, but a long break should help him get back to the sort of form he showed on his hurdling debut, in a maiden at Cheltenham won by another of the fifty, Snap Tie. Quaddick Lake, having travelled well and jumped fluently, led two out but fell at the last where he'd been joined by Snap Tie, the pair clear. There's no doubt that Quaddick Lake, a tall gelding, is up to winning races over hurdles judged on what he showed that day, but it's over fences where his long-term future lies. There's a fair amount of stamina in Quaddick Lake's pedigree—he's by the Jockey Club Stakes winner Blueprint out of an unraced half-sister to the very smart chaser at up to three miles Super Furrow—and he should stay at least two and a half miles.
D E Pipe

Trainer comment: He was very unlucky at Cheltenham but disappointing after, and we just hope it was his fall that was affecting him; he'll stay over hurdles this year.

Qulinton (Fr)

Timeform Rating 127p

4 b.g Bulington (Fr) – Klef du Bonheur (Fr) (Lights Out (Fr))
2007/8 16v* 19m² Apr 26

The Pipe team has enjoyed some wonderful success stories with French imports down the years, and judged on the impression made by Qulinton in a couple of outings in this country there must be every chance of him adding his name to a list that incorporates the likes of Gloria Victis, Cyfor Malta and

Champleve; the last two took advantage of a generous weight-for-age allowance when making their mark as novice chasers, and while young chasers don't get as much help as they once did, it's over fences where Qulinton's future lies.

Successful once from four starts on the Flat for Laurent Viel in his native country, Qulinton justified good support when running out an emphatic winner of a heavy-ground maiden at Plumpton on his hurdling debut. That might not have been a great race of its type but there could be no arguing with the style of the success and it was in a much stronger event that he confirmed himself a useful prospect, at Market Rasen a month later. Whilst narrowly failing to follow up, he battled well in finishing a head second to Ouzbeck, who's gone on to make a very good start over fences. Qulinton remains with the option of novice hurdles until the end of October, whereupon it would be no surprise if connections were to switch him to the larger obstacles. *D E Pipe*

Trainer comment: He's a nice, big horse and he'll make a lovely chaser one day.

Rajeh (Ire)   Timeform Rating 119

5 b.g Key of Luck (USA) – Saramacca (Ire) (Kahyasi)
2007/8 17m* 16d³ 16g² 20gᵖᵘ Nov 24 :: 2008/9 NR (Sep18F)

Bought for 70,000 guineas at the Newmarket Autumn Sales in 2006 after showing fairly useful form on the Flat for Kevin Prendergast, Rajeh initially proved expensive for his new connections following two unplaced efforts over hurdles in 2006/7, the second of which resulted in a £5,000 fine and a twenty-eight-day ban from the Warwick stewards under the non-triers' rule. Victory in a maiden at Market Rasen in early-2007/8 recouped most of those losses and Rajeh has hardly looked back since. He showed further marked improvement on each of his next two starts, his performance when a neck second to Platin Grounds in the Jewson Novices' Handicap Hurdle Final at Cheltenham in October arguably even better than it looked at the time, with the winner going on to acquit himself well off far higher marks in stronger races. Rajeh suffered a breathing problem on his only subsequent start last season, but returned better than ever on the Flat in 2008, winning at Doncaster and Sandown, in the process showing that he has more in the way of stamina than had previously been suspected. The ground could be important to Rajeh, for while he has form on good to soft ground over hurdles he possibly doesn't want it any more testing—all three of his Flat wins have come on good to firm. In view of his efforts on the Flat this year, Rajeh could well have more to offer over hurdles, in which case he will be well worth following in handicap company. *J L Spearing*

Trainer comment: He'll be running if the ground isn't too soft, and we'll look for a race at Cheltenham in October after he ran so well there last season.

Raysrock (Ire)
Timeform Rating 116p F84

6 br. g Anshan – Sovereign Leader (Ire) (Supreme Leader)
2007/8 F17g F16g F16m⁴ 20m² 16v^F 16v* 16s* Apr 7

It's over twenty-five years since Peter Monteith started training but he's never enjoyed as much success as he did last season, when his horses won thirty-four races and putting £1 on all his runners would have resulted in a profit of nearly £40. He did a particularly good job with those sent to him by leading owner David Johnson after they'd rather lost their way for David Pipe, Marcel, Standin Obligation and Commercial Express earning more than £60,000 in winning five times between them, but there were plenty of other owners he won races for, including Alexander Irvine, whose Raysrock ended the campaign by winning novice events over hurdles at Hexham and Kelso. It wasn't as if he was winning out of turn for he ran eleven times before he got off the mark, but he'd certainly been knocking on the door for a while, finishing second on five of his six starts in Irish points and being demoted for causing interference after dead-heating with Logans Run in a maiden hurdle at Musselburgh. His physique and breeding (he's a half-brother to another of the fifty Ballydub) suggest he should prove at least as effective over fences and over further than two miles. *P Monteith*

Trainer comment: He'll have one run over hurdles before going novice chasing; two and a half miles will probably be his trip.

Ring The Boss (Ire)
Timeform Rating 150 c141

7 b.g Kahyasi – Fortune's Girl (Ardross)
2007/8 16v* 16v* 17g⁶ c16d² c16s 20d³ 20g² Apr 26

Second-season novices of Ring The Boss's calibre don't come along very often. In finishing a neck second to Kruguyrova in the Grade 2 Kingmaker

Novices' Chase at Warwick on his first outing over the bigger obstacles, Ring The Boss showed form that certainly entitled connections to have a go at the Arkle Challenge Trophy. In the event, Ring The Boss was patently found out by his inexperience at Cheltenham, but it's very likely he'll prove himself up to competing over fences at that level in time. As it was, Ring The Boss continued his already marked improvement when returned to hurdles with placed efforts in highly-competitive handicaps at Aintree and Punchestown, finishing a neck second to Brave Right at the latter in what was the most valuable handicap hurdle ever staged in Europe. Sky's The Limit proved a good advert for preserving novice status for a second season in 2007/8, winning a couple of Grade 1s in Ireland, and Ring The Boss is sure to win his share of races when sent back over fences. He will stay three miles, and as such connections will have the enviable problem of deciding whether it is another attempt at the Arkle or to go for the Royal & SunAlliance Chase.

P J Hobbs

Trainer comment: He ran well at Warwick and possibly wasn't quite over that at Cheltenham; he wants two and a half miles, or two miles on soft ground, and we're most excited about him.

Ring The Boss promises to prove just as good over fences as hurdles

Rippling Ring (SAF)

5 b.g Saumarez – Rippling Star (SAF) (Fort Wood (USA))
2007/8 16g* 16s⁵ Mar 11

A smart performer on the Flat in South Africa, where he was successful four times at up to a mile and a half, Rippling Ring is probably going to prove at least as good over hurdles judged on the promise he's shown in two runs since being bought by Andy Stewart and sent to Ditcheat. He made an impressive start over hurdles, winning a sixteen-runner novice event at Doncaster in February by six lengths, jumping well, moving smoothly to the front two out and sealing matters in an instant when shaken up. Speed again looked to be his forte in his next race, the Supreme Novices' Hurdle at Cheltenham, which showed just how highly Rippling Ring was regarded by connections. In view of his inexperience he ran a cracker to finish fifth behind Captain Cee Bee, Binocular, Snap Tie and Kalahari King (a horse he'd beaten at Doncaster), travelling strongly for a long way and tiring only as the soft ground took its toll. A good-topped individual who looked in very good condition at Cheltenham, Rippling Ring is the type to make a chaser when the time comes, but there's every chance he'll be able to exploit a potentially very favourable handicap mark over hurdles nearer to hand. *P F Nicholls*

Trainer comment: He ran nicely at Cheltenham and is better now after a summer off; he'll go for 2m handicaps to start with.

Rosbay (Ire)

4 b.g Desert Prince (Ire) – Dark Rosaleen (Ire) (Darshaan)
2007/8 16d⁶ 16d 16s³ Feb 1 :: 2008/9 NR (Sep20F⁵)

Habton Grange Stables has a strong National Hunt tradition, having housed Night Nurse and Sea Pigeon amongst others, and, though known primarily for its Flat horses nowadays, current licence holder Tim Easterby is more than capable of turning out winners over jumps, for all he had just eight last season compared to a best of thirty-two. In Rosbay he looks to have one that could help turn the situation round.

Rosbay had three runs in juvenile hurdles during the winter and made the frame only once, but on each occasion he shaped better than the bare result suggests. Although the BHA handicapper is likely to take no chances with his mark on the back of three encouraging qualifying runs, Rosbay's promise lies in what he's shown on the Flat. Rosbay hasn't won on the level since the summer of 2007, but he's shown himself as good as ever (just about useful) in the most recent season and has regularly been placed in competitive handicaps. If he's able to translate anything like his Flat form to hurdles, Rosbay is a sure-fire winner—on looks he should go as far over jumps as he has done on the Flat. *T D Easterby*

Trainer comment: The plan is to run him wherever the ground is heavy; he was never right over hurdles last season, but he's been in good form on the Flat.

Shalone

Timeform Rating F115+

4 ch.g Tobougg (Ire) – Let Alone (Warning)
2007/8 F16s* F16s² :: 2008/9 F16g* May 3

By the 2001 Derby third Tobougg out of a fair winning miler whose three other foals to reach the racecourse have all won on the Flat, Shalone wasn't given the opportunity to show what he could do in that sphere, but he has proved himself a well-above-average performer in bumpers and, in very good hands, looks to have a bright future over hurdles. Shalone was overlooked by Alan King's first jockey Robert Thornton on his first two starts. Thornton opted for Calafical, who finished ninth, when Shalone made a successful debut at Wincanton in January; and for Charmaine Wood, a remote seventh, when the four-year-old failed by only a short head to get the better of Diamond Harry in the very valuable DBS Spring Sales Bumper at Newbury two months later, claimer Gerard Tumelty again on board. Thornton didn't have a choice to make when Shalone reappeared in a fifteen-runner event at Uttoxeter in the first week of the current season. In the light of Shalone's impressive performance, one in which he matched his smart Newbury form, Thornton must have wondered how he'd ever come to overlook him in his previous races. Under conditions much less testing than at Wincanton and Newbury, Shalone was produced to lead over three furlongs out and quickened so well when shaken up that he put thirteen lengths between himself and his nearest pursuer Little Al, an eight-length winner at Folkestone on his previous start. Shalone isn't an obvious jumper on looks or pedigree, but his stable does get the best out of this type—Katchit is an obvious example—and he looks sure to win novice hurdles this season. *A King*

Trainer comment: Very exciting prospect; he was one of our best bumper horses in the spring and will go novice hurdling now, when we'll start him off at two miles.

Sir Winston (Ire)

Timeform Rating 81+

6 b.g Supreme Leader – Aliandbet Jewel (Ire) (Strong Gale)
2007/8 19d 20s⁶ 24s Apr 12

At first glance Sir Winston hardly appeals as one who will be worth following this season. However, we think he's capable of a fair bit more than he's shown in his three runs over hurdles to date, and though he won't realise his full potential until he goes over fences, we expect his shrewd trainer to find some good opportunities for him in handicap company when he does make the switch. In need of the experience on his debut, Sir Winston finished sixth to the useful Punchestowns in a novice at Uttoxeter on his next start, and then again showed ability when upped to three miles in a maiden there, taking a strong hold and racing prominently until three out. Sir Winston certainly has a jumping pedigree, by Supreme Leader out of a Strong Gale mare, and is chaser on looks, being a good-topped individual. He's been brought along very steadily, and the patient policy adopted with him should start to pay dividends before long. *V R A Dartnall*

Trainer comment: He's had his problems, but we've given him plenty of time.

Snap Tie (Ire)

Timeform Rating 143

6 b.g Pistolet Bleu (Ire) – Aries Girl (Valiyar)
2007/8 16g* 16g² 17g² 16s³ Mar 11

A leading performer in bumpers who might well have reached the top over hurdles had she stayed sound, Aries Girl hasn't enjoyed the same sort of success as a broodmare so far, but that could be about to change. Her fourth foal Snap Tie, who was useful in bumpers, quickly reached that level in his first season over hurdles and will win more races if kept to the smaller obstacles, but this tall gelding looks the type who will prove an even better chaser.

All four of Snap Tie's runs over hurdles took place at Cheltenham. Successful in a maiden on the first occasion, he finished runner-up to I'msingingtheblues then Calgary Bay before going on to show further improvement when stepped up to Grade 1 company in the Supreme Novices' Hurdle. Snap Tie, a 20/1-shot, made headway under pressure to challenge after two out in the Supreme, but he couldn't quicken after a mistake at the last and had to settle for third behind Captain Cee Bee and Binocular. It was the sort of performance Snap Tie's reputation suggested he had in him, and connections think he has prospects of making up into a Champion Hurdle contender. Aries Girl never raced beyond two and a quarter miles but would have stayed further—her dam Ravaro finished second in the 1986 Stayers' Hurdle—and Snap Tie himself seems likely to stay two and a half miles. *P J Hobbs*

Trainer comment: He's likely to run in a two-mile conditions hurdle at Kempton in October; if he wins we'll think about the Champion Hurdle, otherwise it'll be the novice chase route.

Sprosser (Ire)

Timeform Rating c126

8 b.g Alflora (Ire) – Dark Nightingale (Strong Gale)
2007/8 c24d³ c24d* c25g³ c24g* c25m⁴ c21g⁴ Apr 17

The fact Sprosser already looks well treated yet can be expected to improve further when faced with more of a test around three miles, or when stepped up to still longer trips, marks him down as one who should be worth following in handicap chases in 2008/9. A big, rangy, useful-looking gelding, Sprosser had a few runs in Irish points in his younger days (winning once) but has still had only eight races for Oliver Sherwood and will be less exposed than plenty he's likely to come up against in his second season over fences. His two wins in 2007/8 came in small-field novice events but he does have solid runs in handicaps to his name, including when presented with a barely adequate test at Cheltenham in April when, in finishing fourth to Nation State, he came up the hill in the style of one who will relish a return to three miles plus. Whilst unlikely to prove as good over hurdles, Sprosser is still eligible to run in novices over them and should be up to winning an ordinary staying event or two if connections opt to return him to the smaller obstacles at any stage. *O Sherwood*

Trainer comment: We're getting him going early as he likes better ground; he's in good order and jumping is his forte.

The Apprentice (Ire)
Timeform Rating 116 F104

6 b.g Shernazar – Kate Farly (Ire) (Phardante (Fr))
2007/8 F16d* 21s* 19d 21d⁵ 20g⁴ Apr 5

There is every reason to think that The Apprentice can graduate on to significantly better things this season, looking the type who will help further enhance Victor Dartnall's burgeoning reputation. A taking sort physically—one who looks sure to take to fences—The Apprentice appeared a well-above-average prospect when confirming the distinct promise of his bumper debut and winning a similar event at Chepstow in November in good style. His hurdling career got off to a successful start the following month when he was workmanlike in winning a novice at Plumpton. He looked rather inexperienced at several flights on that occasion, and it's fair to say that a lack of fluency hindered him on his three subsequent starts. Despite that he performed with encouragement, notably when fifth to Pettifour in a strong renewal of a well-established Newbury novice, the four to finish ahead of him all going on to win next time. The Apprentice made his handicap debut from a mark of 115. He was unable to land a blow having got behind after early mistakes, but the manner in which he kept on suggested that his mark isn't going to prove insurmountable, with Dartnall having had the time, hopefully, to remedy the flaws in his hurdling technique. Trips in excess of two and a half miles are likely to show The Apprentice in his best light and he's been kept to good ground or softer. *V R A Dartnall*

Trainer comment: He won two races for us last season and jumps fences well, so he'll probably start off in a maiden chase.

The Jazz Musician (Ire)
Timeform Rating 130p F104

6 b.g Tiraaz (USA) – Royal Well (Royal Vulcan)
2007/8 F16s² 21d² 16s* Mar 24

The climax of the opening maiden contest at Chepstow on Monday 24th March had something of a musical theme, the Colin Tizzard-trained The Jazz Musician fully confirming the promise of his hurdling debut when beating I Hear A Symphony by eleven lengths. Hopefully, the impressive winner will be hitting more top notes in 2008/9, whether he remains over hurdles or, as we'd like, he embarks on a novice chase campaign. The son of Tiraaz began his career when occupying the runner-up spot on all three of his outings in bumpers at the same Welsh venue, and he filled the same position on his first attempt over hurdles, when beaten a length and a quarter by another of the fifty Pettifour at Newbury. The form of his win a month later is bordering on useful, and there's almost certainly a fair bit more to come from him. The Jazz Musician is bred to stay beyond twenty-one furlongs, his unraced dam a half-sister to the 1998 King George winner Teeton Mill, though his Chepstow victory showed that he's clearly not short of speed. Hopefully, his handler will be able to compose a suitable programme that will see The Jazz Musician return to the winner's enclosure in the coming months. *C L Tizzard*

Trainer comment: He was bought as a chaser and we'll kick off over fences with him straightaway, probably at Chepstow in the second half of October; then it'll be the Rising Stars Novice Chase at Wincanton if all goes well.

The Pious Prince (Ire)   Timeform Rating – c?

7 ch.g Shahrastani (USA) – Ara Blend (Ire) (Persian Mews)
2007/8 20d^{pu} 20v 19v 25s⁵ 16v :: 2008/9 c23m^{pu} May 6

The Pious Prince has been a flop over jumps to date, but there are reasons for thinking things might finally click with him this season. The Pious Prince was useful in bumpers at his peak, winning twice, but it would have been easy to have lost faith with him over hurdles for Len Lungo so disappointing did he prove last season after shaping as if in need of the run on his reappearance at Carlisle. His chasing debut at Exeter in May was hardly any better despite the fitting of blinkers, but The Pious Prince has started life in handicaps from the mark of a plater and somebody clearly felt he was up to defying it at the first attempt that day judging by support for him in the market. Lungo's success rate has dropped off alarmingly in recent seasons, whereas new trainer David Pipe had as many as a hundred winners in 2007/8, and The Pious Prince could hardly be in better hands with a view to restoring him to his former glories; he's got the potential to run up a sequence in handicaps if he does, with trips short of three miles likely to suit him best. *D E Pipe*

Trainer comment: He's only walking at the minute; he doesn't appear to be overbig, so may be more of a hurdler than chaser.

The Sliotar (Ire)

7 ch.g Presenting – Annie's Alkali (Strong Gale)
2007/8 24g 24g 20d⁶ 20m² 22g* 22d* 21s 24m* :: 2008/9 c24g² May 7

After being granted a permit in 2005, Newmarket-based handler George Haine had to wait until the 2007/8 season to train his first winner outside points. That was Irish recruit The Sliotar, who had been bought out of Mouse Morris' yard in the summer. A winner three times for Haine, The Sliotar has since changed hands again for £75,000 at Doncaster's August Sales and will race in future for David Pipe, for whom he can be expected to progress into a useful staying novice chaser.

Given a break after a strenuous start to his time in Britain, The Sliotar returned in April with his best performance to date. Despite carrying a double penalty in a novice at Southwell, the seven-year-old held off Openditch gamely by half a length having made most of the running. The Sliotar was switched to fences for his most recent outing and was shaping with promise, having pulled clear with the winner Ocean du Moulin, when losing all chance with a bad mistake three out. The Sliotar can be expected to leave that running well behind him for his new trainer and there are clearly races to be won with him over fences, particularly at distances of three miles or more.
D E Pipe

Trainer comment: He'll stay novice chasing; he's an out-and-out stayer and we had our eye on him for a while.

Tot O'Whiskey

7 b.g Saddlers' Hall (Ire) – Whatagale (Strong Gale)
2007/8 20g* 16s* 16v² 24g⁵ 19g 20g³ 20d 19m Apr 26

It could be argued that as both a bumper performer and novice hurdler Tot O'Whiskey rather flattered to deceive. After winning his first three starts in bumpers he struggled to make a significant impact when having his sights raised considerably at Cheltenham and Punchestown. Switched to hurdles last season, Tot O'Whiskey won a maiden and novice at Hexham on his first two outings but failed to get his head in front in six further starts. However, there was more than enough encouragement to be taken from a couple of those runs, notably when third to Beshabar in the EBF Final at Sandown, to suggest that he'll be one to keep faith in when he makes the switch to fences. Indeed, he looks one of the most exciting prospective chasers trained in the North. Tot O'Whiskey has shown that he stays three miles, though is unexposed at that trip, one which may well prove his optimum. Having twice disappointed on good to firm going, it seems fair to assume that he's best on good or softer. **J M Jefferson**

Trainer comment: He'll go novice chasing; he's quick enough for two miles, and there's a race for him at Hexham's second meeting, but he'll probably be better at three.

Trigger The Light

Timeform Rating c127p

7 ch.g Double Trigger (Ire) – Lamper's Light (Idiot's Delight)
2007/8 c24d* c24s* Mar 18

Trigger The Light has long since appealed as one very likely to make a better chaser than hurdler and, though his first season over fences was restricted to just two outings, he won them both and still has plenty of time to prove his true worth over the larger obstacles. His record over hurdles wasn't a bad one by any means, winning twice from a handful of starts and showing a fairly useful level of form, but his physique suggested he'd really come into his own when switched to chasing, and he duly made a winning debut over fences in a maiden at Kempton despite a couple of howlers. Sore shins kept him off the track for nearly four months after that, but he was still able to follow up in a four-runner novice at Warwick, jumping really well for one so inexperienced this time and looking to be keeping something back as he eventually got on top of the runner-up Durante, a length up at the line. Trigger The Light, who has done all his racing on ground softer than good, is likely to benefit from further than three miles, and plenty more improvement can be expected from him in handicaps this season when stamina is at a premium. *A King*

Trainer comment: Unfortunately, he was plagued by sore shins last season, which is why he ran only twice; still unbeaten over fences, though he lacks a little experience so we might start him off in an intermediate or graduation race.

Very Cool

Timeform Rating 133 c102p

6 b.g Sir Harry Lewis (USA) – Laurel Diver (Celtic Cone)
2007/8 17g c22d⁶ 22s 24s* 24d³ 22g* 24s* :: 2008/9 24g² c16g* May 17

Very Cool gave little indication in his first six outings that he was going to live up to the achievements of his two most accomplished siblings, the useful hurdlers Mr Cool and Miss Cool. Blinkers, however, proved to be the making of him as Very Cool began a remarkable run of progress over hurdles thereafter, winning handicaps at Taunton and Sandown before taking an above-average novice event at Newbury. Very Cool was then returned to handicap company in a competitive affair at Haydock, now running off a mark of 130 as opposed to just 99 for his first win, and he showed further improvement to finish a half-length second to Liberate, earning himself a BHA mark of 135.

Crucially, one of Very Cool's first few outings had come over fences, when he finished well held in a handicap at Market Rasen, therefore qualifying him for a separate mark over fences. After his excellent Haydock second, Very Cool re-embarked on his chasing career in a handicap at Uttoxeter, and in winning a steadily-run race over just two miles, without his usual blinkers, he marked himself down as very much a chaser to follow. A game and genuine front runner, Very Cool has been raised to a mark of 107 over fences, but it's very unlikely that will prevent him from winning again, particularly back over a much longer trip. *D E Pipe*

Trainer comment: He improved no end last season when blinkers helped; he gallops and stays yet handled two miles at Uttoxeter.

Viking Rebel (Ire)

Timeform Rating 137p

6 b.g Taipan (Ire) – Clodagh's Dream (Whistling Deer)
2007/8 20v* 20v² 22d* 24d³ Apr 24

Viking Rebel, the winner of a maiden point in Ireland in March 2007, was bought for £120,000 at the Cheltenham Sales the following month and, after just four outings, that's beginning to look money well spent. Sent off a strong favourite at Ayr on his debut over hurdles, Viking Rebel won with the minimum of fuss, and was then arguably unlucky when runner-up under a penalty over the same course and distance. A defeat of the useful Fresh Winter (the pair were a distance clear) at Newcastle quickly saw him back on the winning trail and it wasn't a surprise that connections opted to try him against stronger company in the spring. Admittedly, that came at the Perth Festival—rather than the higher-profile meetings staged at Cheltenham, Aintree and Punchestown—but Viking Rebel still took on a couple of novices with lofty reputations in Lodge Lane and Tazbar. Both proved just too strong for him on the day, but Viking Rebel shaped best for much of the way despite several mistakes and still held a narrow lead at the last when another error ended his challenge. Given that he's very much a chasing type on looks, everything achieved by Viking Rebel last season seems something of a bonus, and he's an exciting prospect for staying novice chases in 2008/9, when he'll be trained by Nicky Henderson following his switch from Nicky Richards' stable. *N J Henderson*

Trainer comment: He's just cantering at the minute; his hurdles form is very respectable and he'll almost certainly go straight over fences.

FINALLY,
A RACING CLUB
LIKE NO OTHER.

The Alan King Interview

Messrs Hobbs, O'Neill and Pipe might have filled the runner-up spot in the trainers' championship in the last three seasons, but Paul Nicholls is in no doubt that Alan King will be his biggest rival over the next few years. King finished third in the 2007/8 championship, topping both the hundred-winner mark and the £2m barrier in total prize money for the first time thanks to the exploits of stable stars Katchit and Voy Por Ustedes, whilst his Barbury Castle Stables are currently home to the largest string of horses amongst jumps-oriented yards listed in the latest edition of Horses In Training. Born into a farming family in Lanarkshire, the forty-one-year-old Scot was a long-time assistant trainer to David Nicholson before briefly taking over the licence at Jackdaws Castle in Gloucestershire upon his mentor's retirement in late-1999. King has been at his current base near Marlborough since the summer of 2000, during which time his rise up the training ranks has been impressively quick— he had fifty-five horses and just eighteen wins in his first full campaign, compared to 183 horses and 128 wins in 2007/8. Nicholls has cited King's plentiful recent supply of successful bumper horses and novice hurdlers as proof that his rival could soon have plenty of ammunition for the bigger prizes on offer over fences. Big-race wins have hardly been in short supply, however, as King has saddled winners at both the Cheltenham Festival and Aintree Festival in each of the last four seasons, whilst Blazing Bailey provided him with his first Punchestown winner (at the first attempt) in April. King can also lay claim to one of the strongest jockey line-ups in the land, with Robert ('Choc') Thornton continuing to thrive in his role as stable jockey, topping the hundred-winner mark himself for the first time last season. Unfortunately, his talented understudy Wayne Hutchinson was forced to miss much of the latest campaign due to a recurring knee injury, but he should be back this autumn, whilst the stable's younger jockeys Jack Doyle and Charlie Huxley both impressed in his absence and appeal as two of the better conditionals around at present. King kindly took time out in September to discuss the prospects of around thirty of his horses for the 2008/9 season.

Bakbenscher   Timeform Rating F115

5 gr.g Bob Back (USA) – Jessolle (Scallywag)
2007/8 F16s* F16s³ F16s* Mar 31

A horse I've always liked. He won two of his three starts in bumpers last season, at Uttoxeter and Wincanton. He was very free when beaten at Chepstow in between and, to be honest, did very well to finish third that day. I know the two horses who beat him are nice prospects but I can assure you that wasn't his true form. Choc was back on board at Wincanton and, having dropped him out, got him to settle beautifully before coming through cantering to win very impressively. We'll go novice hurdling with him now—he's already done plenty of schooling—and will probably start him off over two miles in late-October or November. Hopefully, there'll be some good races in him, as I think he's pretty high class.

Black Jacari (Ire)

3 b.g Black Sam Bellamy (Ire) – Amalia (Ire) (Danehill (USA))
2007/8 NR

A son of Black Sam Bellamy, hopefully he'll prove to be one of our better juvenile hurdlers this season. He's a fairly useful performer on the Flat and, although he's been a little bit disappointing since winning over ten furlongs at Goodwood in May, I half-blame myself for running him on quick ground a couple of times. He's been well schooled and, to begin with, the plan is to follow a similar route with him as we did with Katchit and Franchoek.

Blazing Bailey

6 b.g Mister Baileys – Wannaplantatree (Niniski (USA))
2007/8 25g 24s⁴ 20d* 24d² 24d⁴ 24d* 24g* Apr 24

Grand horse, who enjoyed another tremendous season in 2007/8, winning at Aintree and Punchestown on his last two starts. We put the blinkers on for both of those wins, but I really don't know whether they made any difference at all. He's so tough and genuine, but we just felt it was worth trying something different with him as he tends to hit flat-spots in his races. Having said that, he even hit a flat-spot with the blinkers on—he was going nowhere three out at Punchestown before coming through to win convincingly! Provided he remains competitive over hurdles, he'll contest most of the top staying events again this winter, though I've always felt he'll jump fences in time. I'd imagine he'd follow a similar programme to last season. In an ideal world I'd start him off in the West Yorkshire Hurdle at Wetherby, but that depends on whether they've got the ground sorted out there. Last winter was the first time since I've been training that we didn't have a single runner at Wetherby, which is a real shame as it's a track I've always liked a lot—they really need to get their house in order there.

Call Me A Legend

4 ch.f Midnight Legend – Second Call (Kind of Hush)
2007/8 F13s* F12s⁶ F17d* F17d³ Apr 4

Lovely filly by Midnight Legend who won two of her four starts in bumpers last season. I was delighted with her close third (a place behind stable-companion Divali Princess) in the listed mares bumper at Aintree on her final start, when she was giving weight to the two who beat her. She travelled really well that day and possibly hit the front a shade too soon—Choc said afterwards he'd wished he'd hung on to her for a bit longer. Like all of our bumper horses, she's already done plenty of schooling and will go novice hurdling now. I'll probably start her off in a mares' novice (at two miles), but once she's won I wouldn't be at all worried about her taking on the geldings, particularly as her mares' allowance will nullify any penalty she gets. In any case, she's a very powerful filly and actually looks more like a gelding! I think she's a useful prospect.

Cosmea

3 b.f Compton Place – St James's Antigua (Ire) (Law Society (USA))
2007/8 NR

Together with Black Jacari, Cosmea looks the best of our homegrown recruits to the juvenile hurdle ranks. She's a tough little filly who's done very well for us on the Flat, winning twice this summer before running very well in defeat on both starts since. She'll have no problem staying the trip over hurdles and we've got quite high hopes for her.

Dancingwithbubbles (Ire)　　　Timeform Rating F112

5 b.m Supreme Leader – Kates Charm (Ire) (Glacial Storm (USA))
2007/8 F17s* F16g* F16g^2 Mar 8

Well-bred mare who won bumpers at Folkestone and Southwell last winter prior to getting nailed on the line (beaten a head by Dayia) in the listed mares event at Sandown in March. She was the only one carrying a double penalty that day, so our decision to go to Southwell with her ended up costing us that bigger win. Apparently, they've altered the conditions for the Sandown race in 2009, when there won't be any double penalties. Too late for us! Dancingwithbubbles was still fairly immature last season, so she should be all the better with another summer under her belt. Novice hurdling is the plan.

Divali Princess　　　Timeform Rating F105

4 b.f Muhtarram (USA) – Diva (Exit To Nowhere (USA))
2007/8 F14g^6 F17s* F17d^2 Apr 4

If you watched her at home you'd think she was completely useless. I trained her dam Diva and she was always extremely free, yet this filly is completely different. Nevertheless, she won for us at Taunton on just her second start so we decided to throw her into the deep end in the listed mares bumper at Aintree (when a 40/1 chance). To be honest, she amazed me with her performance there and finished an excellent second to Carole's Legacy, beating our first string Call Me A Legend into third in the process. She's strengthened up a lot since last season and looks far more the finished article, which is encouraging as she'll be going hurdling now. However, I must confess I've no idea how good she might be.

Franchoek (Ire)

Timeform Rating 146+

4 ch.g Trempolino (USA) – Snow House (Ire) (Vacarme (USA))
2007/8 17g³ 16d* 16g* 17g² 16s* 17d* 17d² 20d³ 16g⁴ Apr 26

He spent the summer at J. P. McManus' Martinstown Stud in Ireland and hasn't been back with us all that long, but I'm very pleased with him—I think he's done particularly well physically. He was our leading juvenile hurdler of last season, winning four times, and also ran very well in defeat at both Cheltenham (Triumph Hurdle) and Aintree. He certainly wants at least two and a half miles and I'm looking to go down the World Hurdle route with him—both Crystal d'Ainay and Blazing Bailey were third in that race for us aged five, so I don't think his age should put anyone off. In fact, I actually think he's a classier horse than Blazing Bailey. Not sure where we'll start with

him yet, though it'll certainly be hurdles up until Christmas and then connections will decide which way to go, with fences obviously also an option. Personally, I'd prefer not to go chasing with him this season but we'll wait and see how he fares.

There were few better juveniles last season than Franchoek

Greenbridge (Ire)

6 b.g Luso – Green Divot (Green Desert (USA))
2007/8 F17d 20d^{pu} 17d^2 19d^3 16g* 16d* 16d^6 Apr 4

We've always thought he was very good but he lost his way at the end of his bumper career and took quite a long time to get back on track, possibly down to weakness more than anything else. Anyway, he clicked after Christmas last season and won really well under Jack Doyle in novice hurdles at Doncaster and Kempton (by a distance). He's very much a chasing type and has loved jumping fences at home from day one. We were actually going to run him in a novice chase in May until deciding against it due to unsuitable ground, but he's all set to go again now. I think he could be very interesting for two-mile novice chases.

Halcon Genelardais (Fr)

8 ch.g Halcon – Francetphile (Fr) (Farabi)
2007/8 23s^3 c29s^2 c26d^4 c32g^2 Apr 19

No wins in 2007/8 but enjoyed another good season and was unlucky not to claim a second victory in the Welsh National—the final fence was the only one he met slightly wrong and I'm sure if he'd winged it he'd have held on. He ran another terrific race under top weight when runner-up in the Scottish National, particularly as the ground at Ayr was plenty quick enough for him. The owners don't want him to run in the Grand National, so I'll suppose he'll tackle the Gold Cup again. In truth, he probably hasn't quite got the class to win a Gold Cup, but he's still a very good staying chaser and there aren't any alternatives for him at the Cheltenham Festival. He ran okay to finish fourth in it last season and stayed on very powerfully from three out—he'd just been unable to hold his place as soon as Denman upped the pace with a circuit to go. We've started him off over hurdles in the last few seasons, but he's rated quite highly in that sphere now so I doubt you'll see him over the smaller obstacles again. Instead, I'm toying with the idea of starting him off in the Hennessy at Newbury. He goes well fresh and, with Denman likely to run off top weight, there's a good chance he'll be one of only a handful in the handicap proper.

Howle Hill (Ire)

8 b.g Ali-Royal (Ire) – Grandeur And Grace (USA) (Septieme Ciel (USA))
2007/8 c19g* c16d^4 c16g* c21g^6 c16d c16m^{pu} Apr 26

Has been with us since he was a two-year-old and has been a star from the word go, winning some good races on the Flat as well as over jumps. He picked up valuable handicap chases at Ascot and Doncaster last season, but now figures on a BHA mark of 151 so he won't be easy to place in 2008/9. He's another horse who is best when fresh, so I'll have to do my homework to try and find him a good race to start off in. I know the ground at Ascot hasn't been to everyone's liking since the course reopened in 2006 but, fortunately, it rides better than it walks and is getting better year by year— touch wood, horses do seem to come back from it okay. Howle Hill, for example, had been off for thirteen months prior to his win there last autumn and went on to have a good season.

Il Duce (Ire)

8 br.g Anshan – Glory-Glory (Ire) (Buckskin (Fr))
2007/8 c20g* c20g^2 c21g^{pu} c20d^{pu} c21d^2 :: 2008/9 c22d^{pu} Jul 19

I kept him in training for the Summer Plate at Market Rasen, but that proved to be a complete waste of time—they just went off far too quickly for him early on and he was soon off the bridle. He had a late summer holiday after that run and, given that Cheltenham seems to suit him, he'll probably return in the Paddy Power Gold Cup in November (runner-up at 33/1 in 2007). However, he looks very exposed off his current mark in my opinion. He got hammered for that second place to L'Antartique in last year's Paddy Power and then went back up the weights after chasing home Stan back at Cheltenham in the spring. On top of that, he's a very hard horse to catch right and I'm never sure how he's going to run—you think he's in great form but then he lets you down and vice versa!

The blinkered Junior goes close in the Coral Cup

Junior   Timeform Rating 138

5 ch.g Singspiel (Ire) – For More (Fr) (Sanglamore (USA))
2007/8 20d 20d² 20d³ 20d Apr 3

Interesting horse for 2008/9. He only joined us in the second half of last season and ran well on all three starts, including when third in the Coral Cup at Cheltenham. He's still a novice, which does give us plenty of options for the new season and, ideally, I'd love to get a couple of confidence-boosting wins into him before tackling some better races later on. Instead of running on the Flat, he's had a proper summer break this time and I'm sure that will have done him the world of good. We'll start him off at around two and a half miles, but I'm confident he'll stay further in due course (stays well on the Flat).

Katchit (Ire)

5 b.g Kalanisi (Ire) – Miracle (Ezzoud (Ire))
2007/8 16d* 16d³ 17g² 16g* 16s* Mar 11

I'm afraid to say he hasn't grown any since last season! Having said that, he's done nothing but improve ever since he's joined us (from Mick Channon) and now works like a really good horse at home. I don't know whether that's just because he's got stronger with age or if it's a confidence thing from all his wins—he's now won ten out of thirteen starts over hurdles. I've got his 2008/9 campaign mapped out except for his starting point. He reappeared in a four-year-old contest at Aintree last autumn, which obviously isn't an option this time around, and at the moment I'm leaning towards the Elite Hurdle at Wincanton in early-November as his first race. We're giving the Fighting Fifth at Newcastle a miss this season (third to Harchibald in 2007). The owners wanted to go there last season because of the £1m bonus on offer but, in my opinion, it probably cost us a win in the International Hurdle at Cheltenham on his next start (when runner-up to Osana). Therefore, we'll be going straight for the International after his reappearance, and then turn him

The remarkably tough Katchit (star on cap) isn't to be denied in the Champion Hurdle

out again fairly quickly for the Christmas Hurdle at Kempton. As in 2007/8, we'll give him a short break before warming up for the Festival in the Kingwell at Wincanton, and then it'll be back to Cheltenham to defend his crown in the Champion Hurdle. I know there are one or two decent novices from last season to contend with this time around, but he's tremendously tough and certainly won't give up his title without a fight. He loves Cheltenham, after all.

King's Revenge

Timeform Rating 131

5 br.g Wizard King – Retaliator (Rudimentary (USA))
2007/8 16g^4 16g^2 16s^4 16m^3 16d 19g^4 17d 16s^3 17g^3 Apr 18

He's been a grand horse for us, but I'd love to see him get his head in front again. He went up a fair bit in the weights last season without winning, which always gets a trainer questioning himself if he's done something wrong! King's Revenge did, however, pick up plenty of prize money in 2007/8 thanks to seven finishes in the frame, most of which came in very good handicap company, and he's clearly a useful performer. We might start him off in another handicap hurdle, but I'd imagine we'll go down the novice chase route with him after that, which will hopefully increase his winning opportunities.

Mount Helicon

3 b.c Montjeu (Ire) – Model Queen (USA) (Kingmambo (USA))
2007/8 NR

One of two juvenile hurdle prospects we've got off the Flat from Andre Fabre in France, the other being Saticon. We're very excited about both of them. Mount Helicon has won twice this year, whilst he's also made the frame three times in listed or Group races, showing form at up to fifteen furlongs. He could be very good.

My Way de Solzen (Fr)

Timeform Rating 158 c137

8 b.g Assessor (Ire) – Agathe de Solzen (Fr) (Chamberlin (Fr))
2007/8 c23s⁵ c24dᵖᵘ 20d² 24d⁵ 20g⁶ Apr 5

One of our few downsides to last season was My Way de Solzen. We obviously had very high hopes for him but he had a most disappointing season, including when reverted to hurdles and tried in blinkers. I haven't been able to find any physical problems with him to explain his loss of form, so the big task is to try and get him back to being competitive again. Who knows if he'll bounce back? All I can say is that he oozes class at home and seems to be in very good form after a long break this summer. I'm going to come back down in trip with him this season, and hopefully that will help. Provided the ground is right, we might well start him off at around two miles in the Haldon Gold Cup at Exeter and take it from there. I've never been convinced that he's a proper stayer anyway. I know he won the World Hurdle in 2006, but he was rolling about on the run-in that day and I'm not sure he really stays that sort of trip. We'll be keeping him over fences from now on and let's hope the drop in trip works.

Nenuphar Collonges (Fr)

Timeform Rating 144

7 b.g Video Rock (Fr) – Diane Collonges (Fr) (El Badr)
2007/8 21v² 24g* 21v² 24d* 24d⁴ :: 2008/9 21d May 25

He's a very tough horse, but he's just so bloody cautious when it comes to jumping—he's so careful and spooky, even over hurdles! It's certainly not for the lack of schooling, as he's literally jumped hundreds and hundreds of obstacles at home. He's still been a real star since joining us, winning three times over fences in 2006/7 and then enjoying a tremendous season back over hurdles in 2007/8, winning the Grade 2 Bristol Novices' and the Grade 1 Spa Novices'—it's possibly no coincidence that both of those wins came on Cheltenham's New Course, which has only two flights of hurdles in the final three-quarters of a mile. He'll almost certainly go back over fences now, with races such as the Welsh National on the agenda. My only fear is that his slow jumping might just hinder him given the handicap marks he's now got to run off.

Oh Crick (Fr)

5 ch.g Nikos – Other Crik (Fr) (Bigstone (Ire))
2007/8 20m⁶ 17s² 16v* 17d* 17s* 17g* 16g :: 2008/9 c19d* May 1

Did nothing but improve last season and won four on the trot over hurdles, including a competitive handicap at Hereford on the final occasion. He was a bit over the top when scraping home on his chasing debut back at Hereford in May, but he was always going to win that day and Choc did take things fairly easily. Although that win was over nineteen furlongs, I'd be inclined to drop him back to two miles for his return this autumn. Indeed, we're hoping Oh Crick and Greenbridge can take a pretty high rank in the novice chase division at that trip. Handicap chases could also be an option for him later in the season. Fortunately, the way he wins his races—he tends to prick his ears when getting to the front and is never going to win by far—means he's the kind of horse the handicapper may struggle to get a hold of.

Old Benny

7 b.g Saddlers' Hall (Ire) – Jack's The Girl (Ire) (Supreme Leader)
2007/8 24d² 23s c24v³ c24v² c24d² c32d* c32g⁴ Apr 19

One of our three Cheltenham Festival winners last season, when he broke his duck over fences in the four-mile National Hunt Chase under Charlie Huxley. He also ran another sound race when fourth in the Scottish National at Ayr on his final start. Unfortunately, he got injured in a field whilst summering with his owner Mr Hemmings and isn't back with us yet. Therefore, plans are very much up in the air with him at present and, if he does run in 2008/9, it will be after Christmas. I know Mr Hemmings likes to have runners in the Grand National but, even before his injury setback, I felt Old Benny would want another year before tackling that race.

Orion d'Oudairies (Fr)

6 b.g Grand Tresor (Fr) – Quelinda (Fr) (Pot d'Or (Fr))
2007/8 F16d F16s 16s^F 21d^3 :: 2008/9 22g* May 3

He fell three out on his hurdling debut and then finished third to Pettifour in a very good novice there in late-February. We decided to keep his novice status intact for this season, and he duly won a novice at Uttoxeter shortly after the 2008/9 campaign had begun. In truth, he made fairly heavy weather of that win but, as in the case of Oh Crick's chasing success, he was probably past his best by that stage. He looks a stayer in the making and, although probably not one of our top novices, he should still win more races.

Pouvoir (Fr)

5 gr.g Verglas (Ire) – Policia (Fr) (Policeman (Fr))
2007/8 16d^2 16m^4 16d^2 21g* Dec 15

An exciting novice chase prospect. He suffered a very slight problem after winning the Relkeel Hurdle at Cheltenham in December, which is why he wasn't seen out again in 2007/8. He's fine now and has grown again in the interim. He actually hasn't done any schooling yet, but I don't see that being a problem—he's a big, imposing horse who should have no trouble taking to fences. To be honest, Pouvoir is a horse I've always thought the world of and it was frustrating that he kept getting beaten last autumn. The form of those defeats proved to be very strong, however, and the step up in trip seemed to really help him at Cheltenham. We'll start him off in a novice chase at around two and a half miles and I think he'll have no problem staying three miles in time. I'm very hopeful for a good season with him.

Pur de Sivola (Fr)

5 b.g Robin Des Champs (Fr) – Gamine d'Ici (Fr) (Cadoudal (Fr))
2007/8 c16g^2 c21v* c16d^2 c16s* c20g^F c19d^4 Mar 27

A big, powerful gelding who suffered with sore shins last season, which explains why he sometimes didn't look in love with the game. That was certainly the case when he disappointed at Exeter on his final start—I shouldn't really have run him there and he's a lot better than that form suggests. I actually thought he'd have won the Pendil Novices' Chase at Kempton on his previous start but for taking a very heavy fall three out. He'd won twice at Wincanton prior to that, which is a course which takes some jumping, so I wouldn't write him off yet. He could be a contender for the Paddy Power Gold Cup at Cheltenham in November.

Saticon

3 b.g Act One – Saumareine (Fr) (Saumarez)
2007/8 NR

I always enjoy the juvenile hurdlers as you can run up a sequence with them, which you just can't do with the older novices nowadays. We do a huge amount of schooling with them and tend to get them out fairly early in the season, which was a policy my old boss David Nicholson used to adopt. Saticon would be one of our biggest juvenile hopes at this stage for 2008/9. Along with Mount Helicon, he's come to us from Andre Fabre after showing useful form on the Flat in France, winning his last two starts at Longchamp and Chantilly this summer.

Shalone   Timeform Rating F115+

4 ch.g Tobougg (Ire) – Let Alone (Warning)
2007/8 F16s* F16s² :: 2008/9 F16g* May 3

Another very exciting prospect. He could be anything! In truth, he only shows an adequate amount of ability at home—he doesn't burn the gallops up or anything like that—but he was one of our best bumper horses in the spring and will go novice hurdling now. He's actually a Flat-bred gelding but was probably too green for that—he was unsold at the Breeze-Up Sales as a two-year-old before I bought him twelve months later. In fact, he did race a little bit green in his only defeat to date, when beaten a short head by Diamond Harry in a valuable bumper at Newbury, so I suppose it could be argued he should still be unbeaten. He was certainly most impressive when winning at Uttoxeter next time and should win his share over hurdles this season, when we'll start him off at two miles.

Squadron   Timeform Rating 125

4 b.g Sakhee (USA) – Machaera (Machiavellian (USA))
2007/8 16s* 17d³ 16g² 16s 17d* Apr 16

Kept some good company as a juvenile hurdler last season, when he won at
Sandown and Cheltenham. His second place to Crack Away Jack at Sandown
in between doesn't look too bad now given he was conceding 10 lb to that
horse, whilst I actually thought he ran very well for a long way in the Fred
Winter at Cheltenham—I know he finished well down the field in the end,
but Choc did look after him once he was held. We'll keep him over hurdles
for the time being and at around two miles to begin with, though he should
stay further if required. He was a pretty good stayer on the Flat for Amanda
Perrett, after all.

Theatre Girl   Timeform Rating 132

5 b.m King's Theatre (Ire) – Fortune's Girl (Ardross)
2007/8 16m* 16s² 16g² 20d⁵ 18g* Apr 10

She's a mare who's done particularly well since last season. I'd like to think
there might be some improvement to come, just from a physical viewpoint,
as she's certainly a lot stronger this time around. She won two novice hurdles
last season, but also pushed Chomba Womba very close at Doncaster and
wasn't disgraced when fifth in the David Nicholson Mares' Hurdle at the
Cheltenham Festival, which turned out to be a much stronger contest than I
thought it was going to be. She'll have her campaign geared around the series
of listed and graded races now on offer to mares, with the Cheltenham race
again her main target. I'm all in favour of these new mares' races. It gives
owners and breeders a chance to keep mares in training or, in some cases,
even put mares into training, which wouldn't necessarily have been the case
before. Ideally, I'd like to start Theatre Girl off in the mares race at Wetherby
in early-November but, as I said earlier, that all depends on whether they've
sorted the ground out there for this season.

The Hairy Lemon

8 b.g Eagle Eyed (USA) – Angie's Darling (Milford)
2007/8 17g⁵ c19m^F 21g⁴ c18s* c20d⁴ c19s* c20g* c20d Mar 13

Enjoyed a cracking first season over fences in 2007/8, winning three times, including handicaps at Taunton (beating Roll Along a short head at level weights) and Kempton. He was blinkered for those two wins and really seemed to improve for the fitting of headgear—he's not ungenuine, it's just that he can be very hard work in his races. He's crept up the handicap (now rated 138 by the BHA), so I'm not sure where we'll start this season. I'm half-toying with the idea of running him back over hurdles, as he had a mark of 113 when last seen in that sphere, though it all depends on what the handicapper does under this new system of taking other form into account. Nenuphar Collonges, for example, was campaigned solely in handicap chases in 2006/7 and ran off some fair marks too, yet his chase rating has been raised as a result of his exploits over hurdles since.

Trigger The Light

7 ch.g Double Trigger (Ire) – Lamper's Light (Idiot's Delight)
2007/8 c24d* c24s* Mar 18

A thorough stayer. He's one of those horses that doesn't do an awful lot once he hits the front, but he's a good sort and just could be alright. Unfortunately, he was plagued by sore shins last season, which is why he ran only twice. It's quite unusual for one of our older horses to suffer from sore shins—you expect it more from two-year-olds and bumper horses—but he was affected by them after his wins at both Kempton and Warwick. Anyway, he looks very well at present, and is still unbeaten over fences. He lacks a little experience and, as he's no longer a novice, we might look to start him off in an intermediate or graduation chase.

Valleyofthedolls

Timeform Rating F95p

4 b.f King's Theatre (Ire) – Fortune's Girl (Ardross)
2007/8 NR :: 2008/9 F16m* May 11

We've got another huge team of bumper horses for the new season and, to be honest, it's too early to say which ones are likely to prove the best amongst that group. Having said that, I'm looking forward to seeing Valleyofthedolls again on the racecourse. She met with some setbacks last season and didn't make her debut until this May, when winning a mares' bumper at Uttoxeter despite racing very green. She's a sister to Theatre Girl—the two of them come from a very good jumping family—and seems sure to go on to better things.

Voy Por Ustedes (Fr)

Timeform Rating c170

7 b.g Villez (USA) – Nuit d'Ecajeul (Fr) (Matahawk)
2007/8 c16s² c16s² c16d* c17d² c16d² c20d* Apr 4

It's going to be interesting to see how he gets on this season, as we'll be starting him off at longer trips from the outset. He's actually never been the quickest at home and has probably been crying out for a step up in trip—he certainly seemed to relish it when gaining his revenge over Master Minded in the Melling Chase over two and a half miles at Aintree. Having won the Queen Mother Champion Chase in 2007, we obviously felt obliged to defend that crown last season. However, given the manner in which Master Minded had beaten him at Newbury, it was always on the cards we'd have to play second fiddle to that horse again at Cheltenham. Anyway, Voy Por Ustedes is in very good form at present and will probably return to Aintree for his reappearance in the two-and-a-half-mile Old Roan Chase in late-October. Then it may be the Peterborough Chase at Huntingdon followed by a tilt at three miles in the King George VI Chase at Kempton on Boxing Day. We'll just see what happens there and decide where to go with him after that. I suppose we might be tempted back to two miles if something happened to Master Minded, but the Ryanair Chase must definitely come into the equation now as a Cheltenham Festival target. He's been ultra consistent for us and is a remarkably tough horse. Regardless of how many hard races he has, he always comes back for more and he's been a joy to train—we could do with a few more like him

Voy Por Ustedes (pink cap) gains revenge on Master Minded at Aintree

The Graham Lee Interview

There is surely no one who would begrudge Graham Lee a change of fortune given what he has gone through this year. Lee had already ridden eighty-nine winners and was second only to A.P. McCoy when a fall from Cash King at Huntingdon in February led to an injury-enforced absence of almost three months; and just as things were getting back on track for him—a little over two months after winning the Swinton Hurdle at Haydock on Blue Bajan in fact—another spill, this time at Worcester, caused him to miss the second half of the summer with concussion. Lee describes 2008 as a 'nightmare,' but admits he cannot wait to get back to work, and he's pencilled in late-September for his return having recently been working regularly with the fitness coach of Middlesbrough F.C.. Lee missed out on fourteen winners for retainer Ferdy Murphy alone during his lay-off in 2007/8, and riding more than a hundred in a season for a second time looks a very real possibility this time around such is the ammunition at his disposal, not just from Murphy but other yards, too. He kindly took time out recently to discuss some of those he hopes will contribute to his chase for a second century, as well as expressing his view on the Denman and Kauto Star rivalry.

Aces Four (Ire)

9 ch.g Fourstars Allstar (USA) – Special Trix (Ire) (Peacock (Fr))
2007/8 c25m^{pu} 24m^5 Mar 9

I believe he's okay. I think the boss is going to aim him at the Peterborough and then the King George. I pulled him up in the Charlie Hall but was very pleased with him as he just got tired very quickly. He didn't do much over hurdles at Market Rasen after when Ewan Whillans rode him, but he's a chaser and I'd easily forgive him that. He's a very good jumper and he's got a bit of pace as well, and he's one I'll really be looking forward to riding.

Big Burrows (Ire)

6 b.g Supreme Leader – Bula Vogue (Ire) (Phardante (Fr))
2007/8 F16v^3 F17g^4 F16g^5 Apr 19

His head is the size of a Ford Transit—he's a lovely, big horse. Settling him has been important, and when A.P. (McCoy) rode him at Ayr he said two and a half miles will be ideal over hurdles. He wants bringing along quietly and slowly and we'll have some fun with him. He'll be a chaser in the future.

Blue Bajan (Ire)

6 b.g Montjeu (Ire) – Gentle Thoughts (Darshaan)
2007/8 16g^2 16d* 16d* 16d 16s^6 16d^2 :: 2008/9 16g* May 10

I'm unbeaten on him, three from three. His jumping has got better and better—at Leicester he bolted up but his jumping was average—but I always felt he'd jump more fluently off a faster pace and he was impressive in the Swinton. He wants a good pace with as much cover as you can get and the Haydock race worked out so well, putting a lot of distance between himself and the rest after the last. I'd love to think he could bridge the gap, and something like the Elite or the Kingwell Hurdle at Wincanton would tell us a lot more. Katchit's a loveable little thing, but he's not a great horse and if something comes along who's improving he's there to be shot at.

Caipiroska
Timeform Rating 112p c118

9 b.g Petoski – Caipirinha (Ire) (Strong Gale)
2007/8 c24g* c20m² c20g⁴ c25g² c24m* 20g² c21dᵘʳ 19s* c28v³ c22s³ Feb 14

When the race works out and I can keep holding on to him he looks very impressive, but if the chips are down half a mile out and you're having to work on him you've no chance. He'd have a right chance in a three-mile handicap at the Aintree meeting because he'll relax and jump and the faster the pace the better for him.

Coe (Ire)
Timeform Rating 131

6 br.g Presenting – Dante's Skip (Ire) (Phardante (Fr))
2007/8 20m⁵ 19d³ 23d* 20v* 24g² 24d³ 24d Mar 14

He didn't know what he was doing when I won on him at Wetherby, but the ability was always there. I was most pleased with him in defeat at Doncaster, as he was off the bridle a long way out on ground that was too quick for him and he was so tough. He's probably a soft ground horse, and I think he's a chaser in the making.

Kalahari King (Fr)
Timeform Rating 138

7 b.g Kahyasi – Queen of Warsaw (Fr) (Assert)
2007/8 20g³ 16d* 16g⁴ 16d² 16s⁴ 16g³ 20g* Apr 24

He's a gorgeous horse, a natural—he's got lots of pace and is a very accurate jumper of a hurdle. I believe he's going novice chasing this season, and the type of jumper he is over hurdles I think now would be the time because three years down the line he just might not get what's required. I don't see any reason why it (chasing) wouldn't work, but if it doesn't he can go back hurdling with something like the totesport Trophy in mind.

L'Antartique (near side) and Graham Lee team up successfully at Cheltenham for a second time

L'Antartique (Fr)

Timeform Rating c150

8 b.g Cyborg (Fr) – Moomaw (Akarad (Fr))
2007/8 c20d* c20g* c24d⁶ c17d⁴ c20d Mar 13

He didn't stay for me in the Lexus the last time I rode him. He's a good horse, and for him to be a Cheltenham Festival winner in the Jewson and then come back and win a Paddy Power was a great effort. I really enjoy riding him because he's not the most natural jumper and Ferdy (Murphy) has him so well schooled—I've no doubt he wouldn't have won those races if he'd have been in many other places. Without speaking to Ferdy, I'd say the Ryanair would be his long-term aim.

Naiad du Misselot (Fr)

Timeform Rating 136p

7 b.g Dom Alco (Fr) – Une Nuit (Fr) (Le Pontet (Fr))
2007/8 24d 20s* 20d* Mar 14

He's going chasing. He's a tough, professional, straightforward sort of horse and was a natural jumper over hurdles. The fact is he's a Cheltenham Festival winner and I think anything could be possible with him even though he's not a big, robust horse.

Negus de Beaumont (Fr)

Timeform Rating c121

7 b.g Blushing Flame (USA) – Givry (Fr) (Bayolidaan (Fr))
2007/8 c24v² c24vᶠ c20v⁴ c33dᵖᵘ Feb 23

He won five times over hurdles in 2006/7, and I like him a lot. I rode him one day over fences at Sedgefield last season, but he didn't go a yard—he's a grinder, and if you keep digging he'll keep finding. He could be one for something like the Welsh National or the Eider in time.

New Alco (Fr)

Timeform Rating c148

7 b.g Dom Alco (Fr) – Cabira des Saccart (Fr) (Quart de Vin (Fr))
2007/8 c20g* c26vᵖᵘ c21g c24s² c25g⁵ Apr 23

I rode him out the other morning and he feels fantastic. He won his prep last year at Carlisle and didn't figure in the Hennessy, so with his record fresh we're going to go straight to Newbury. How you ride him doesn't really matter—he's a very, very straightforward horse—and it might be an idea to take Denman on for the lead if he runs as he'll be giving us so much weight.

Nine de Sivola (Fr)

7 b.g Video Rock (Fr) – Quine de Chalamont (Fr) (Do Do (Fr))
2007/8 NR

I rode him out the other day and he looks absolutely fantastic. He's rated something like 140 with a second in an Eider, an Irish National and a Scottish National to his name, yet is still a novice. He's got loads of experience, is a very good jumper and, though I don't know Ferdy's plans, he could well be a National horse.

Pakineo Des Pictons (Fr)

5 b.g Kadalko (Fr) – Akinea (Fr) (Royal Charter (Fr))
2007/8 F16s* Nov 21

Since he won his bumper at Hexham he must have grown two inches. He does everything like a proper horse—he gives you a good feel and is well balanced—and I was so pleased with what he did in his bumper because if you look at Ferdy's record we don't do bumpers. I would hope he could be a graded novice hurdler this season.

Supreme Builder

7 b.g Supreme Leader – Osocool (Teenoso (USA))
2007/8 20d 24v⁵ 16d 20s* 22v* :: 2008/9 24d³ May 2

He's a big so-and-so and has an awful lot of natural ability. Put it this way, it's there and Ferdy will bring it out slowly. I rode him at Newcastle over three miles and said he needed dropping in trip so he could learn to settle. That worked, and we started stepping him back up and got him back on side, but it could be two more seasons before he fulfils his potential.

The Duke's Speech (Ire)   Timeform Rating 124 c95x

7 b.g Saddlers' Hall (Ire) – Dannkalia (Ire) (Shernazar)
2007/8 16g⁴ 16m c21s⁵ c16d³ 16g⁶ 16g :: 2008/9 17g⁶ May 16

He had a few runs over fences for Tom Tate and it wasn't good. He didn't jump well when we got him, but, like L'Antartique, we schooled him and schooled him until it became second nature, and I was delighted with him when he ran at Fakenham only for him to let me down at Musselburgh. It's just a case of channelling his ability and if he could put his head in front he'll put three or four together.

Three Mirrors   Timeform Rating c148

8 b.g Cloudings (Ire) – Aliuska (Ire) (Fijar Tango (Fr))
2007/8 c20m⁴ c20g c22s⁶ c16dᵖᵘ c25d² c20d* Apr 18

Ferdy mentioned to me he might go for the Paddy Power, but I don't know if he's a horse who wants sun on his back given he's gone and won at Ayr for the last two years. He's a very quick jumper but, if you put a gun to my head, I'd say he wouldn't be quite good enough for it. I hope I'm wrong!

Three Mirrors is one Lee will be hoping to be reunited with in 2008/9

Tidal Fury (Ire)

6 b.g Night Shift (USA) – Tidal Reach (USA) (Kris S (USA))
2007/8 19s² 19s* c17mᵖᵘ 19sᵖᵘ c17d c18gᵖᵘ Apr 12

I had a sit on him recently and he moved well and felt good. He was Champion three-year-old in France, and with Ferdy's track record (with those he inherits from other stables) I'd be really excited about him. He wants proper winter ground I think.

Water Taxi

7 ch.g Zafonic (USA) – Trellis Bay (Sadler's Wells (USA))
2007/8 c16g² c16m² c17s* :: 2008/9 c16d c17m² c16g² c20g² c20g* Aug 3

When we started schooling him over fences he was absolutely brilliant and he went on to be placed on his first three starts in chases, but then he ran at Leicester and the fences were a disgrace—he got two inches down into one and paid the penalty. He was shot to bits after that, but he's been intensively schooled since and it's clicked with him again, as his results have shown.

Denman vs Kauto

I would ignore the Gold Cup. I would have sided with Ruby all day long and ridden Kauto Star. I don't think Kauto Star jumped with his usual slickness and I thought for him to get as close as he did going to the second last was an amazing effort. Denman will be favourite now as well. The only horse that has really taken Denman on was our horse, Aces Four, in the SunAlliance and we were going every bit as well as him when we did the splits at the third last, so maybe that's the way to beat him.

Apt Approach (Ire)

5 ch.g Bob Back (USA) – Imminent Approach (Ire) (Lord Americo)
2007/8 F17s* F16d⁶ F16g Apr 23

The annual guessing game amongst punters as to which of Willie Mullins' bumper horses is 'the one' has long been a regular feature of the Irish National Hunt season, and last term the proverbial dogs were barking the name of Apt Approach throughout the winter months. When the son of Bob Back eventually made his debut on soft going at Gowran in mid-February, he did not disappoint his supporters, winning impressively by fourteen lengths in a race that worked out very well. As it turned out, Mullins had in his stable the best bumper horse since comprehensive figures for such races were first published by Timeform in the 1993/4 season, but it wasn't Apt Approach. Still, he wasn't discredited behind the horse in question, Cousin Vinny, in the Grade 1 bumpers at the Cheltenham and Punchestown Festivals, faring best of those that raced close to the pace when sixth at the former course. A point winner in all but name (he fell at the last when well clear on his only start in that sphere), Apt Approach is out of an unraced half-sister to the 1996 Irish Grand National winner Feathered Gale and hails from an excellent jumping family that also includes his connections' remarkable servant Adamant Approach. He can be expected to stay at least two and a half miles and rates as a smart novice hurdling prospect. *W P Mullins*

Arc Bleu (Ger)

7 ch.g Monsagem (USA) – Antala (Fr) (Antheus (USA))
2007/8 17d* 16d :: 2008/9 20m² May 7 (Jul28F³)

Arc Bleu is potentially the best-treated hurdler in Ireland and with one of the top men in the business at plotting a course through handicaps. The German-bred gelding returned to his useful best on the Flat in 2008, becoming the first Irish-trained winner of the Northumberland Plate in June, and showed no ill-effects from that hard race when third to Majestic Concorde in a prestigious amateur handicap at Galway the following month. Arc Bleu has been lightly raced over hurdles so far, but won with considerable ease on his handicap debut in early-2007/8, and is totally unexposed at trips beyond two miles. His only run over further was at Punchestown in May, when he failed to justify short-priced favouritism but did well the way the race was run in going down by two and a half lengths to Roamanob on good to firm going, travelling strongly held up then staying on without being able to get in a blow at the all-the-way winner, who followed up next time. Arc Bleu, who is currently rated just 104 over hurdles, may not be fully effective on heavy going, but is a winner on soft on the Flat. He could run up a sequence in handicaps, working towards a valuable prize in the spring, with the Coral Cup (a race his trainer won in 2003 with Xenophon) appealing as a suitable target. *A J Martin*

Carrigeen King (Ire)

Timeform Rating 118 c102p

7 b.g Beneficial – Carrigeen Kerria (Ire) (Kemal (Fr))
2007/8 F16v* c20v^F 20d^2 :: 2008/9 c20s^2 May 1

The small family set-up run by Dick Lalor in County Tipperary has been very well served by the 'Carrigeen' line. Carrigeen Kerria, out of the useful two-mile to three-mile chaser, Carrigeensharragh, was a fairly useful handicapper over fences for the stable in the mid-'nineties, and Dick's wife Anne has already bred three winners out of her. The first of them, Carrigeen Victor, was trained by Jessica Harrington to win the Grade 1 Dr P. J. Moriarty Chase in 2005, but second foal, Carrigeen Kalmia, was retained by the Lalors and has proved just as talented, winning four races in the capable hands of their daughter, Liz, including a listed chase at Thurles in 2007. Liz also rides Carrigeen King, who became Carrigeen Kerria's third winning foal when landing a bumper at Clonmel in December. The son of Beneficial was pulled up in a couple of points in 2006 and finished only sixth on his hurdling debut the following year, but he did it decisively at Clonmel, seeming to idle as he pulled three and a half lengths clear of next-time-out winner No Toll. Carrigeen King showed fairly useful form when overhauled only close home by Front Man in a decent maiden hurdle at Thurles in March, but chasing is going to be his game, and he put a first-fence fall at Punchestown (prior to Thurles) behind him when runner-up to Paolo Soprani at Tipperary in May. That form is nothing special, but Carrigeen King jumped soundly and, as a big, substantial type, should be suited by a more galloping track. He'll stay beyond two and a half miles and should have little difficulty winning a maiden chase before perhaps making up into a useful handicapper. *R H Lalor*

Carrigogunnell (Ire)

Timeform Rating 126p F81

6 ch.g Fourstars Allstar (USA) – Ahead of My Time (Ire) (Royal Fountain)
2007/8 F18v³ 20v* Feb 6

Carrigogunnell Castle in County Limerick was once a stronghold of the mighty O'Brien clan, but ended up in the hands of Cromwellian forces during the siege of Limerick and was blown apart in 1691. The castle remains in ruins, but the Carrigogunnell trained by Charles Byrnes hopefully has his best days ahead of him. The six-year-old son of Fourstars Allstar was backed into joint-favouritism for a maiden at Down Royal on his hurdling debut in February and created a lasting impression in beating Brotenstown easily by two and a half lengths. Carrigogunnell looked different class to the opposition for most of that two-and-a-half-mile contest, travelling strongly before leading three out, and the runner-up boosted the form later in the season, winning twice at Limerick, including a decent mares event. There were three other subsequent winners behind Carrigogunnell at Down Royal, and he looks sure to pay his way in the coming season. He'll really come into his own when sent over fences and upped to three miles if looks and pedigree are anything to go by. His brother Five Seven Live has won points and hunter chases, while his dam is also a winning pointer and a half-sister to the dam of the fragile but high-class staying chaser Eurotrek. Carrigogunnell may not be the easiest to train, either, as he has been restricted to just two runs so far (third in a bumper at Limerick on his debut in December), but is in excellent hands and has time on his side. *Charles Byrnes*

Cooldine (Ire)

Timeform Rating 154

6 b.g Beneficial – Shean Alainn (Ire) (Le Moss)
2007/8 16d³ 19s⁴ 18s* 22v* 22v* 20d* 20s* 24g⁴ :: 2008/9 21d May 25

When Ted Walsh referred to Archie O'Leary as a 'lucky old owner' live on RTE television, O'Leary reputedly asked his trainer Willie Mullins to tell Walsh that 'I am neither lucky nor old'. While O'Leary is entitled to quibble over the second point, there is no doubt that he and his wife Violet, in whose name their horses run, have enjoyed a good deal of success with the likes of Florida Pearl and Missed That, and the couple look to have another potential star chaser on their hands in Cooldine. A smart performer in bumpers,

Top novice chasing prospect Cooldine (spots on cap) wins again

Cooldine's hurdling career got off to a stuttering start, with defeats at Cork and Limerick in December, but he never looked back after the turn of the year, especially when his stamina was tested. By the end of March he'd completed a five-timer, which included a couple of Grade 2 wins. The first one was gained with ease at Thurles, but he had to work harder for the second under a penalty at Fairyhouse, where he got the better of a good tussle with Chasing Cars by three quarters of a length, though the pair were fifteen lengths clear of the remainder. Cooldine topped those efforts, and those of any other novice hurdler in 2007/8, on his first venture into open company, when fourth to Blazing Bailey in the Grade 1 World Series Hurdle at the Punchestown Festival, leading briefly after two out before fading to be beaten eleven lengths. He finished only eighth in the Prix La Barka on his final outing in May, but may have been feeling the effects of a hard season or a long journey, so that run is probably best overlooked. Cooldine, out of a sister to useful staying chaser Brackenfield, and already a point winner, will reportedly go straight over fences when he reappears, and is surely a candidate for top honours in staying novice chases. *W P Mullins*

Dooneys Gate (Ire)

7 b.g Oscar (Ire) – Park Breeze (Ire) (Strong Gale)
2007/8 c24d* Mar 6

A lightly-raced seven-year-old, Dooneys Gate has undoubtedly been difficult to train, but he has made the most of the limited opportunities he has had, winning three of his four starts, including a bumper at Wexford and a well-contested maiden hurdle at Fairyhouse in 2006. Dooneys Gate missed the following year, and returned in March to make his chasing debut in a maiden at Thurles. He made hard work of getting the better of Parrot Cay by half a length in an ordinary race in which only half the sixteen-strong field completed, taking longer than the runner-up to respond to pressure before staying on to get on top close home. The form is nothing special but Dooneys Gate can't get much of a mark on the basis of that run, and has an excellent pedigree for a staying chaser, as a brother to Offshore Account, a smart novice in 2006/7, and a half-brother to several useful or better jumpers, notably multiple Grade 1 winner The Listener. Dooneys Gate wasn't seen again last season and his novice status has now been sacrificed, but his trainer

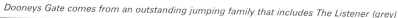

Dooneys Gate comes from an outstanding jumping family that includes The Listener (grey)

reports all to be well with him, and he is an interesting prospect for staying handicap chases on going softer than good. *W P Mullins*

Grancore Girl (Ire)   Timeform Rating F114

5 b.m Flemensfirth (USA) – Raise An Ace (Buckskin (Fr))
2007/8 F17s² F16s* F16v* Mar 15

A full sister to the useful hurdler Black Harry, Grancore Girl doesn't have the impressive physique of her rangy sibling, but she certainly doesn't lack for ability, and will have a good season over hurdles if her bumper form is anything to go by. Having made an encouraging debut when second to Apt Approach at Gowran in mid-February, she duly built on that effort to win a twelve-runner event at Clonmel in good style a fortnight later. However, it was her performance in a useful bumper at Limerick thirteen days on from Clonmel that really stamped Grancore Girl as a smart prospect. Ridden confidently on heavy going, she had plenty to do over two furlongs out, but made up ground very stylishly to lead in the final furlong and kept on strongly to win by eight lengths from Rating Queen, with a couple of next-time-out winners back in third and fourth. While Grancore Girl is lacking in size, she is quite a lengthy type and looked rather unfurnished when our reporter saw her at Limerick, so she should have filled out after a summer out at grass, which was reportedly the plan. By Flemensfirth, she'll stay at least two and a half miles and should take a bit of beating in novice races confined to mares. *Thomas Gerard O'Leary*

Joncol (Ire)   Timeform Rating F106

5 b.g Bob's Return (Ire) – Finemar Lady (Ire) (Montelimar (USA))
2007/8 F18v* F19d² Feb 24

When the useful chaser Colnel Rayburn was plying his trade for Paul Nolan earlier this millennium, he was reputed to be the tallest horse in training in Ireland, standing just under 18 hands. While not quite so large in stature, the 17.2 hands Joncol looks to be a more than able substitute for Nolan in the 'talented brute' category. Joncol came good at the second attempt in points when accounting for two subsequent winners in December, and just under two months later made a successful racecourse debut when ploughing through heavy going to win a sixteen-runner bumper at Thurles by eight lengths from Definitive Edge. He made only one subsequent appearance, showing stamina and gameness in abundance to make the useful Gonebeyondrecall pull out all the stops in a nineteen-furlong bumper at Naas in February. Nolan reports that Joncol has done particularly well during the summer months and will go straight over fences this season. He looks sure to stay three miles and his ability to handle heavy going should help to ensure he wins his share of races. *Paul Nolan*

Miss Fancy Pants

Timeform Rating 116p

4 gr.f Act One – Sweetness Herself (Unfuwain (USA))
2007/8 16m² 16s* 16d² 16g Apr 26 :: 2008/9 NR (Jul28F⁶)

Having shown no better than fair form on the Flat at two and three, Miss Fancy Pants was a low-profile recruit to hurdling for Noel Meade in 2007/8. She took to the new discipline well, though, and after winning a juvenile maiden at Navan in March, went down by only a neck to Paco Jack in a Grade 3 at Fairyhouse, before making little impact in a Grade 1 on her final start. Even on that form, she should be able to take advantage of a Turf Club mark of 110, and she improved further in handicaps back on the Flat in the summer, winning at Naas before following up in the Ladies Derby at the Curragh. She took the latter event in impressive style by three and a half lengths, and had subsequent Galway Hurdle winner Indian Pace back in third. A daughter of Irish Cesarewitch winner Sweetness Herself, Miss Fancy Pants ought to stay beyond two miles over hurdles, but is a strong-travelling sort and gives the impression she may not be suited by a slog. *N Meade*

Oscar Rebel (Ire)

Timeform Rating 132p F–

6 b.m Oscar (Ire) – Be My Baltic (Be My Native (USA))
2007/8 16v³ F16v⁶ 18d* 20s* 18g* Apr 26

When Grangeclare Lark was retired in January with a leg problem, she bowed out the winner of six of her last seven starts over hurdles, including the valuable Grade 3 mares events at the Fairyhouse and Punchestown Festivals the previous season. Those races would probably have been on her agenda again, but she'd have had her work cut out to beat Oscar Rebel, who took both of them in tremendous style. Oscar Rebel looked no better than modest to start with. She won a point in November, but only at the third attempt, and finished third on her hurdling debut in December before being well beaten in a bumper later in the month. She proved a totally different proposition in the spring, completing a hat-trick by an aggregate of twenty lengths, putting up her best display at Punchestown on her final start, when she gave weight to all of her rivals and ended the unbeaten record of the runner-up Serpentaria in most convincing style. Oscar Rebel, who is "very ordinary at home" according to her trainer, is reportedly to be sent over fences this season and should make at least as good a chaser as hurdler. If she does, then some of the listed and Grade 3 events confined to mares could be hers for the taking. Her unraced dam was out of the useful chaser at up to three miles Baltic Brown, and Oscar Rebel will also stay beyond two and a half miles. *W J Burke*

Our Bob (Ire)

Timeform Rating 131 F103

6 gr.g Bob Back (USA) – Mondeo Rose (Ire) (Roselier (Fr))
2007/8 F16g^2 18v^4 F16d^4 19s* 20d^3 18d^4 Feb 10

Trevor Hemmings needs a new flag bearer in Ireland after the retirement of his Grand National winner Hedgehunter and the fatal fall suffered by Our Ben in January. Our Bob, from the same stable, could be the one to fill the void. The grey son of Bob Back was nothing special in bumpers, winning only one of five starts, but quickly developed into a useful novice hurdler in the early part of this year. He won a maiden at Naas with some authority, then finished in the frame in a couple of graded events at Leopardstown, including when beaten only a length and a half into third by subsequent Spa Hurdle runner-up Liskennett over two and a half miles. A tall, lengthy gelding, Our Bob is very much a chasing type in appearance and should stay well—his dam was a winning chaser and fair hurdler at up to three miles. *W P Mullins*

Smoking Aces (Ire)

4 b.g Old Vic – Callmartel (Ire) (Montelimar (USA))
2007/8 F16s* F16s² Apr 6

Smoking Aces was bred to do well in bumpers, being a half-brother to Roll Along, who went through his three starts in that sphere unbeaten, and if things had panned out differently, Smoking Aces could also be going jumping with an unblemished record. Ridden by his owner's son, JP Magnier, the four-year-old made the perfect start to his career with an impressive win in a twelve-runner event at Thurles in mid-February, quickening nicely off a steady pace to prevail by three lengths from Healys Bar. The Champion Bumper at Cheltenham was mentioned as a possible target, but instead Smoking Aces went for a bumper at Limerick in early-April. He lost little caste in defeat there in going down by a length and a half to Galant Ferns, with a gap of ten lengths back to the third, as the winner got first run and Smoking Aces closed steadily even though Magnier dropped his whip over two furlongs out. Smoking Aces was put away after that, but will reportedly return in the autumn, and should have a good season over hurdles. Roll Along ran his best race when runner-up in the Royal & SunAlliance Chase in March and Smoking Aces, by Old Vic, is also going to stay well beyond two miles. Their dam was a half-sister to Nahthen Lad, who twelve years earlier had gone one better than Roll Along in the Cheltenham race. *T J Taaffe*

Solwhit (Fr)

4 b.g Solon (Ger) – Toowhit Towhee (USA) (Lucky North (USA))
2007/8 16s* 16d⁵ 16g* Apr 23 :: 2008/9 NR (Sep20F)

If there was a table which measured success at hitting the target when the money is down, Charles Byrnes would be near the top. Therefore, the bookies must have been quaking in their boots when cash poured on Solwhit for a four-year-old hurdle at the Punchestown Festival. Solwhit came into the race a relatively-unknown quantity after only three runs, the first two of which were for Belgian trainer Claude Dondi, and included a hurdles win in blinkers at Enghien in November. Solwhit's debut for Byrnes came just eleven days before Punchestown, and he caught the eye keeping on into fifth behind

Serpentaria at Fairyhouse. Bookmakers' fears were realised at Punchestown, as Solwhit took care of a large field with something in hand, following Silverhand through after two out and leading approaching the last to beat that one by four lengths. The form looks very solid for a race of that type, as the next three home had already shown fairly useful form and the fifth has done subsequently in handicap company. Solwhit justified further heavy support in a fourteen-furlong minor event at Killarney on the Flat in May, showing plenty of pace, and his shrewd trainer can be relied upon to exploit a Turf Club hurdles rating of 125. Expect Solwhit to win at least one decent handicap in the coming season, probably at two miles. *Charles Byrnes*

Summer Seeds (Ire)   Timeform Rating 83p c102p F77

5 b.g Fruits of Love (USA) – Sophie May (Glint of Gold)
2007/8 F16g 16s c24d⁶ c24sᶠ c20s³ c17s² Mar 24

A Turf Club mark of 96 makes Summer Seeds a must for this section. This strapping son of Fruits of Love kept good company in novice and maiden chases last season, and looks to have got into handicaps lightly on his placed runs at Naas and Fairyhouse in March. He's only a five-year-old, probably still finding his strength, and was considerably handled by Gary Hutchinson on his three completed starts over fences. Summer Seeds suffered a heavy fall at Navan in March, but has generally impressed with the fluency of his jumping for one so inexperienced, his size enabling him to negotiate most fences without breaking stride. His last run, when he went down by eleven lengths to the useful Reisk Superman at Fairyhouse, was over seventeen furlongs, but he saw out two and a half miles well the time before and his dam, Sophie May, was a fair chaser at up to three and a quarter miles in Britain. Summer Seeds, fitted with a tongue strap on all starts over fences, has raced only on good ground or softer so far. *T M Walsh*

Total Excitement (Ire)   Timeform Rating F114

6 b.g Michelozzo (USA) – Oak Court (Ire) (Bustineto)
2007/8 F16d⁵ F16v⁴ F19d* F16g⁶ :: 2008/9 F16d² May 5 (Aug8F*)

The 2004 Champion Bumper winner Total Enjoyment never got the chance to fulfil her potential over hurdles, injuring a knee following her third run over them, after which she developed laminitis and met a premature end. Her half-brother, Total Excitement, hasn't had the same success in bumpers, but he strikes us as a similarly speedy type, the sort to do well over hurdles when there is little emphasis on stamina. He eventually got off the mark at Cork in March on his fourth start, and showed useful form when sixth to Cousin Vinny in the Grade 1 at the Punchestown Festival, before putting up a display of similar merit when runner-up to Uimhiraceathair at the Curragh in May. At the last-named track, Total Excitement typically travelled very strongly held up and looked all over the winner as he made smooth headway to lead under two furlongs out, only to tie up inside the last. That wasn't the first time Total Excitement lost a race he looked to have in the bag, and he's definitely more a 'bridle horse' than a 'grinder'. With that in mind, it could be that his novice hurdling campaign will mirror his bumper one, and that he won't be seen to best effect until the spring when the ground is generally less testing. He has been kept on the go on the Flat through the summer and looked well suited by the sharp thirteen furlongs at Wexford when landing the odds in good style in a maiden in August. *Thomas Cooper*

Champion Bumper winner Total Enjoyment, whose hurdling career was cut short by injury

The Willie Mullins Interview

The 2007/8 season proved to be a tremendous one for Willie Mullins, who topped the table in terms of winners and prize money in Ireland and enjoyed success at the highest level with J'Y Vole (Dr P. J. Moriarty Novices' Chase) and Cousin Vinny (Champion Bumpers at Cheltenham and Punchestown). Timeform's Kevin Blake went to visit Mullins in August at his stables at Bagenalstown in the south-east of Ireland, and the Champion Trainer was kind enough to share his thoughts and outline his plans for many of his team. Here's what he had to say:-

It was great to win the championship last season. We had a good summer by our standards then the horses tapered off in the autumn, as they always do, before coming back into form for the winter. Thankfully, the good form lasted all the way through to Punchestown. Most of my horses are not long back in and the vast majority will be geared towards getting to the racecourse in October/November. We have room for 100 horses here and, as the season goes on, plenty will come in and out. We ran about 130 individual horses last season and it will probably be much the same this time round.

Older Horses

Candy Girl (Ire) Timeform Rating 117 c138

9 b.m Un Desperado (Fr) – Dynamic Venture (Ire) (King's Ride)
2007/8 20d^3 c24s^F c18d^2 c22v* c20s^2 c24s* Apr 6

She has always shown plenty at home and I could never understand how we didn't win a bumper with her. She is another difficult horse to ride, but seems to have found her way over fences. She's had little bits of injury trouble, which is why she is quite lightly raced, but we minded her because we thought a lot of her and it's paying off now. Her owner is keen to go for another season and we'll look for more black type over fences for her.

Ebaziyan (Ire) Timeform Rating 152

7 gr.g Daylami (Ire) – Ebadiyla (Ire) (Sadler's Wells (USA))
2007/8 16g^4 16s^5 20v^3 16d^4 20v* 16d^5 16s 24d 16g^3 Apr 25

He'll be back earlier than most, as I think he may prefer better ground, so he should be out by early-October. I was disappointed with his performances last term, but sometimes horses that have achieved so much as novices will disappoint and then come back to form the following season. We'll probably send him chasing this time around, maybe after a run over hurdles first. I considered running him back on the Flat but don't think I'll go down that road with him until next year, if at all.

Emma Jane (Ire) Timeform Rating 118 c128

8 b.m Lord Americo – Excitable Lady (Buckskin (Fr))
2007/8 c20d^2 c20v^3 c20v^5 c21v^F 19s^6 c19d* c25g* Apr 26

She came to us after her fourth start last season, and I was delighted with her progress. I thought she might have lost her confidence a bit in the jumping department, so we ran her over hurdles and that seemed to help her to come right, as she won both her chases afterwards. I was hoping to have her ready for the Galway Plate, but she had a little setback. She will run in staying handicaps, and graded mares chases will be open to her if she can improve a bit.

Freds Benefit (Ire)   Timeform Rating c134

7 ch.g. Beneficial – Welsh Ana (Ire) (Welsh Term)
2007/8 c17v* c20s^F c16s^3 c21s* c20s^2 c17s^{pu} c24s^5 c18g* Apr 23

He's done very well out at summer grass this year. His pedigree would suggest he wants three miles plus, but he's such a good jumper that he can win at two. He's a difficult horse to ride, in that he races freely, and maybe he's just more straightforward over shorter trips, at which we can let him bowl along and use his good jumping. I'm still convinced, however, that if he settles into his game he will win a big race at around three miles. Sometimes, when they get older, they mellow a bit, so I'm hopeful that he will do just that.

Glencove Marina (Ire)   Timeform Rating 145 c149p

6 b.g Spectrum (Ire) – Specifiedrisk (Ire) (Turtle Island (Ire))
2007/8 21s 20v^4 c20d* c21v* Jan 13

He had a slight tendon injury last season and, while it hasn't been decided yet, I think he needs the year off. I have a very high opinion of him, but he was only injured this year and I'd be happy enough if he comes back in eighteen months time. I don't think there is anything to be gained in rushing him back.

Jayo (Fr)   Timeform Rating 143

5 ch.g Grape Tree Road – Joie de Nuit (USA) (Affirmed (USA))
2007/8 16s* 16d^4 16v^5 16d 19s* 20g^3 :: 2008/9 21d^5 25d Jun 22

He is another difficult horse to ride: if he gets any daylight, he races much too freely. I think there is a big handicap hurdle in him, but I think I will send him chasing this season. He's a fine big horse and should have no trouble jumping fences.

J'Y Vole, who won her first three starts over fences

J'Y Vole (Fr)

Timeform Rating 121 c132

5 b.m Mansonnien (Fr) – J'Y Reste (Fr) (Freedom Cry)
2007/8 19s* 19s c20v* c20v* c21d* c20d³ c16g³ :: 2008/9 25d Jun 22

She had a good campaign in 2007/8. For me, her performance to win the Dr P. J. Moriarty Novices' Chase at Leopardstown was one of the performances of the season among my team. I think she'll stay three miles, but I also feel she has the speed and jumps quickly enough to come back in trip. She is versatile regarding riding tactics, so we can ride her as required, whatever the trip and ground is. She is a tall, narrow mare and, while she has strengthened over the summer and will continue to mature, I think that is how she will always be when race fit. I think she should win another Grade 1 contest.

Pomme Tiepy (Fr)

Timeform Rating c132

5 b.m Apple Tree (Fr) – Unetiepy (Fr) (Marasali)
2007/8 c17s² c17d* c20v* c24d* c24d* c24dᶠ c25g² :: 2008/9 c29d c22dᶠ Jun 22

She was a pleasant surprise last term. She was bought as a nice prospect from France, but we didn't dream she would make into a graded winner so quickly. I know she got all the weight allowances as a young mare, but I think she is well above average for her sex and she'll improve again this season now that we know her a lot better. We had a late season with her, as she ran in France shortly after the end of the Irish campaign, and she is only just back in so probably won't be seen out until November/December.

Scotsirish (Ire)

Timeform Rating 134 c144

7 b.g Zaffaran (USA) – Serjitak (Saher)
2007/8 c22v² c18d³ c17g³ c17v* c17sᶠ c16d³ c16s c21g* :: 2008/9 21d May 25

He has plenty of gears, but the way he won his last start in 2007/8 off top weight in a handicap at the Punchestown Festival, and being by Zaffaran, we will look to experiment more with longer trips this season and we think he will stay three miles. We have had all his family going back three generations and they were basically good ground horses. But that isn't essential for this horse, and he acts on soft going as well.

A step up in trip is the plan for Scotsirish this season

Snowy Morning (yellow colours) puts up a bold display in the Grand National

Snowy Morning (Ire)

Timeform Rating 142p c160

8 b.g Moscow Society (USA) – Miss Perky (Ire) (Creative Plan (USA))
2007/8 c26v^F 18s* 20s* c24d^3 c25d^3 c36g^3 c25g^2 Apr 23

I imagine he'll be entered in the Aintree Grand National, but I don't think that will be his main target. We geared his whole season towards it in 2007/8 and he couldn't win it off the weight he had. So, off a stone higher mark, I don't think it would be worth putting our eggs in one basket with him. He'll be entered in all the top chases at around three miles and we'll take everything as it comes with him.

Novice Chasers

Black Harry (Ire)
Timeform Rating 143p

8 b.g Flemensfirth (USA) – Raise An Ace (Buckskin (Fr))
2007/8 NR

He will make his return from injury this season and will be a bit later appearing than most, with Christmas time being a rough estimate. I won't run him until he can get real winter ground, and he'll go chasing. I always thought he had huge potential. I didn't run him in the bumper at Cheltenham as he was so big and immature. I thought everything went right with him until he raced too freely in the Brit Insurance Novices' Hurdle and fell at the last. He then got some leg trouble off the back of it. We've given him plenty of time off and hopefully he'll come back to his best.

Cooldine (Ire)
Timeform Rating 154

6 b.g Beneficial – Shean Alainn (Ire) (Le Moss)
2007/8 16d³ 19s⁴ 18s* 22v* 22v* 20d* 20s* 24g⁴ :: 2008/9 21d May 25

I'm looking forward to him going over fences this season. He is an out-and-out stayer that was bought from the point-to-point field, but he's not slow, either, and was sharp enough to win a bumper. He handles soft ground better than most, but I don't think he needs it bottomless. We were always happy with his hurdling, but his previous owners always maintained that whatever he did over hurdles would be a bonus, as he is a much better jumper of a fence. I'm hoping they are right!

Fiveforthree (Ire)
Timeform Rating 148p

6 gr.g Arzanni – What A Queen (King's Ride)
2007/8 16s* 20d* 16g³ 20g² Apr 25

I think we may have to go chasing with him, but I don't know: could he be Champion Hurdle material? I made up my mind to go chasing with him during the course of last season, but when a horse goes and wins over hurdles at the Cheltenham Festival, as this one did, the temptation is to keep them over the smaller obstacles. That said, I often think too many horses stay hurdling when they should go chasing, so I'm fairly sure I'll take the latter course with him. He's obviously an exciting prospect, especially as he's bred to stay every inch of three miles. He has done more than most of my horses at this stage, but we will be in no rush to get him out.

Quatre Heures (Fr)

Timeform Rating c116

6 b.g Vertical Speed (Fr) – Macyrienne (Fr) (Saint Cyrien (Fr))
2007/8 c17v² c18s³ Feb 16

He is a bit injury prone and I won't be rushing him. If I can keep him right, he looks an exciting prospect, but he's quite hard on himself and we'll just hope he stays sound. He has plenty of gears and will probably prove best around two miles.

Taipan's Way (Ire)

Timeform Rating 112p F97

6 b.g Taipan (Ire) – Wayward Bride (Ire) (Shernazar)
2007/8 F16g² F20mˢᵘ F16g² F19g* F16m² F19g² 20d 16d* 20g Apr 24

He'll probably have a run over hurdles, but he's a chaser in the making and we won't be hanging around over timber for long. He tends to sweat quite a bit, but it isn't something to be too concerned about. He is also quite a gross horse and is the type to need a few runs to get fully fit. He could well reappear earlier than most of mine, with September being a rough estimate.

Uncle Junior (Ire)

Timeform Rating 132 c105

7 b.g Saddlers' Hall (Ire) – Caslain Nua (Seymour Hicks (Fr))
2007/8 F19d* F17d* 16m³ 24d⁵ 20m² 22g* 20d* 22d* 24d² 24d 20g⁵ ::
2008/9 25dᵖᵘ c22g² c22g⁴ Jul 31

He was a bit disappointing on his second start over fences at Galway in July, but you have to remember that he was a very slow learner over hurdles and it looks like he'll be the same in chases. He will learn his trade the hard way, but he certainly has an engine, and when he gets the hang of things he could find himself well handicapped. He's on a break at the moment and will be brought back later in the season, though he wouldn't want real winter ground.

Second-Season Hurdlers

Quevega (Fr) — Timeform Rating 126

4 b.f Robin Des Champs (Fr) – Vega IV (Fr) (Cap Martin (Fr))
2007/8 16s* 16s* 16g :: 2008/9 19d³ Jun 22

I imagine she'll stay hurdling this year. She developed very well physically and is very strong now—built like a tank you could say—for all that she isn't the biggest. I think she will prove best on a soft surface, and, while she should stay at least two and a half miles in due course, I'm in no rush to step her up.

Serpentaria — Timeform Rating 121

4 b.f Golden Snake (USA) – French Spice (Cadeaux Genereux)
2007/8 16d* 16d* 18g² Apr 26 :: 2008/9 NR (Jul 28F)

I think she will make into a nice staying hurdler. However, she jumps well enough and has enough size and scope to go chasing. At the moment, I only have hurdling on my mind with her, but we might be open to a re-think after Christmas when we will be able to see how much she has improved. She's from a well-established staying family on the Flat and should come into her own when tackling staying trips over jumps.

Shakervilz (Fr) — Timeform Rating 130 F92

5 b.g Villez (USA) – Zamsara (Fr) (Zino)
2007/8 F16v* F20d⁴ F16v⁵ 20s² 20g* 24s* 24g³ Apr 23

He took a surprisingly long time to come to himself but has progressed into a very nice staying hurdler. We are in two minds about what to do with him this season. He needs to improve only a bit to be competitive in the top staying hurdles, but he jumps fences well. We could go novice chasing, but it

---

wouldn't be a problem to come back for the World Hurdle at the Cheltenham Festival. He progressed so much last season, I've no reason to believe he won't improve further. It looks as though we're going to have plenty of novice chasers this year, which makes it all the more tempting to stay over hurdles with this horse.

Novice Hurdlers

Apt Approach (Ire)   Timeform Rating F120

5 ch.g Bob Back (USA) – Imminent Approach (Ire) (Lord Americo)
2007/8 F17s* F16d⁶ F16g Apr 23

He is likely to go over hurdles, though we could go straight over fences with him, as Eddie Hales, who we bought him off, feels he will be a completely different horse over them. I think he prefers soft ground, even though he is bred to act on good. Staying chasing will be his game eventually.

Ballyhaunis

3 b.c Daylami (Ire) – Ballet (Sharrood (USA))
2008/9 NR

This is a lovely horse, who won on the Flat at the Curragh in July. The trouble he gave at the start at Sligo, when losing his chance by whipping round at the tape, was unexpected and probably just down to inexperience: it is unlikely to happen again. Since then he has run well to finish third in a listed event over a mile and three quarters at the Curragh , and how he fares on the Flat for the remainder of the season will dictate whether he goes over hurdles this season or next. He should do well when he does, as he has schooled very well.

Cousin Vinny (Ire)   Timeform Rating F134

5 b.g Bob Back (USA) – Trixskin (Ire) (Buckskin (Fr))
2007/8 F16s* F16d* F16g* Apr 23

He's back in now and will go hurdling. I was slightly surprised how well he acted on good to soft and good ground at Cheltenham and Punchestown considering he went so well on what was almost unraceable ground at the latter course on his debut. He seemed to travel better at the Cheltenham Festival than at the Punchestown one, but I think the reason for that was that they went a slower pace at Cheltenham and he did everything very easily there, while at Punchestown they went that bit faster early. Another factor was that I was quite hard on him in the build-up to Punchestown, as I wasn't happy with him. He disappointed me in a few pieces of work after Cheltenham, and I began to think I had given him too easy a time after that run, so I did plenty with him and he eventually came right. Normally I don't turn my Cheltenham bumper horses out again after that run, and I have had a few disappointments in the Punchestown bumper, so it is to his credit that he improved again there. He has an electric change of pace and I don't imagine we will need to go further than two miles with him. He jumps hurdles very well and, to look at him schooling, you would have to think of him as a chaser for the future. Obviously, we are very excited about him.

Hurricane Fly (Ire)   Timeform Rating 133p

4 b.c Montjeu (Ire) – Scandisk (Ire) (Kenmare (Fr))
2007/8 NR :: 2008/9 16m* 19d* 19d^2 Jun 22

He had three runs over hurdles shortly after the end of the 2007/8 season, winning at Punchestown and Auteuil and finishing second in a Grade 1 at the latter track, and is a very exciting prospect. We'll probably geld him in the next few weeks and won't rush him back. The Royal Bond Novices' Hurdle at Fairyhouse in November would be a tentative first target and the Supreme Novices' Hurdle at the Cheltenham Festival would be an obvious longer-term target. However, despite his pedigree suggesting otherwise, I think this horse will stay well and the Ballymore Properties Novices' Hurdle could well be an alternative.

Lilywhitedancer (Ire)   Timeform Rating F115

6 b.g King's Theatre (Ire) – Relief Map (Relkino)
2007/8 F16g* F16d^5 F16g :: 2008/9 F16d May 5

He showed tremendous ability on what I thought was soft going when winning on his debut, and is likely to prove best on that sort of ground over hurdles. He will probably race at around two miles for the time being and should be out in October.

Meath All Star (Ire)
Timeform Rating F105p

5 ch.g Presenting – Seven Ages (Ire) (Topanoora)
2007/8 NR :: 2008/9 F16g* Jul 11

He always looked a nice sort and the form of the bumper he won—at Cork in July—is working out well. He's on a little break at the moment and will appreciate good going. He should win another bumper before he goes hurdling.

Quiscover Fontaine (Fr)
Timeform Rating F99p

4 b.g. Antarctique (Ire) – Blanche Fontaine (Fr) (Oakland (Fr))
2007/8 F16g* Apr 22

We had his half-brother, Kim Fontaine, who was a really nice staying hurdler. Unfortunately, he had legs like glass and never realised his potential, but this horse could well make up for that. He's a hardier, stronger horse with better conformation. He certainly isn't as flashy a worker as his brother, as he showed very little at home before he won the Land Rover Bumper at Punchestown, but the racecourse obviously brings out the best in him. He was the first off the bridle in that race and he responded very well to forge on and win, despite running green and idling in front. He is a stayer in the making and I am looking forward to running him over hurdles.

Sir Vincent (Ire)
Timeform Rating F106

5 b.g Norwich – Another Partner (Le Bavard (Fr))
2007/8 F17g :: 2008/9 F16d* F17g* Jul 14

He is a nice prospect that has won both his starts in bumpers for me this season, at Sligo and Killarney. He is on a short break at the moment, having just come back from the sales. His immediate future is over hurdles, but he is a chaser in the making. He acts well on good ground.

Themoonandsixpence (Ire) — Timeform Rating F105

5 ch.g Presenting – Elphis (Ire) (Supreme Leader)
2007/8 F16s² F16d³ F18m* :: 2008/9 F16d⁵ May 5

He is another nice hurdling prospect that is ultimately a chaser in the making. He acts well on better going and will hopefully be out in early-October in search of that sort of ground. Three miles should be no problem to him in due course.

Uimhiraceathair (Ire) — Timeform Rating F116

6 b.g Old Vic – Petrea's Birthday (Ire) (Buckskin (Fr))
2007/8 F16g³ F16v* F16g⁴ :: 2008/9 F16d* May 5

He is another that has shown more on the track than he has at home, winning at Navan and also at the Curragh, the latter shortly after the end of the 2007/8 season. He'll go hurdling this season, but is a staying chaser in the making. Soft ground is a big help to him.

Bumper Horse

Quel Esprit (Fr)

4 gr.g Saint des Saints (Fr) – Jeune d'Esprit (Fr) (Royal Charter (Fr))
2008/9 NR

He was one of the highest rated point-to-pointers in Ireland last season, winning his only start at Dundrum, and we bought him off Willie Slattery, who we also bought Cooldine off. He is a very big horse and looks a promising sort. He will hopefully run in a bumper at around Christmas time.

Potential Improvers

Equus Maximus (Ire)

8 b.g Flemensfirth (USA) – Sambara (Ire) (Shardari)
2007/8 19s 20s³ 20d² 19d* 24g Apr 24

This is a really talented horse that has had some leg trouble. He looks very well at the moment and is sound. I think he's one to follow over fences this season.

Golden Silver (Fr)

6 bl.h Mansonnien (Fr) – Gold Or Silver (Fr) (Glint of Gold)
2007/8 21d⁵ c20s² c20s⁶ 19s 19sᵖᵘ 19s c19s 24g Apr 24

He's a lovely chasing sort that was bought from France. He had shown useful form over hurdles there, but I didn't have him fully ready for his only run for me thus far at Punchestown. He's much better than he showed that day and will win races.

The Timeform View From Ireland

The 2007/8 season was one of mixed fortunes for Irish stables and points to the likelihood of more of the same in the campaign to come. Irish-trained horses won seven races at the Cheltenham Festival (compared to nine, ten and five in the preceding three years), but that did not include success in any of the big four contests—the Champion Hurdle, Cheltenham Gold Cup, Champion Chase and World Hurdle—for the first time since 2001/2. At the same time, British-based runners regularly plundered prizes in Ireland, including half of the ten Grade 1 events at the Punchestown Festival.

Things might have been slightly different had not **Sizing Europe**, the horse with the best one-off performance of the season over hurdles in Ireland, seemed to go wrong in the Champion Hurdle itself and missed the remainder of the campaign. Sizing Europe's easy defeat of **Hardy Eustace** and **Al Eile** in the AIG Europe Champion Hurdle at Leopardstown in January saw him go off a short-priced favourite at Cheltenham, but he went from going well to going nowhere in a matter of strides after two out. The good news is that Sizing Europe is said to have recovered (he was a probable for Punchestown for a long time), and he will stay over hurdles for the time being. His best is slightly better than Katchit's best in our book.

The previous year's Champion Hurdler, **Sublimity**, failed to win in 2007/8 but could still be a potent force for a while yet, especially if he can make it to the racecourse a bit more often. His three runs in the latest campaign included a fourth to Katchit in the Champion Hurdle at Cheltenham and a second, when ridden with little enterprise, to Punjabi in the Punchestown equivalent.

Most of the other leading Irish hurdlers had seen better days or fallen slightly short of high class, with **Kazal** doing best of the stayers by following a win in the Boyne Hurdle at Navan with a third to Inglis Drever in the World Hurdle at Cheltenham. The tough and reliable **Aitmatov** was second to Kazal in the Boyne and sixth at Cheltenham before doing best of the home contingent when third in the World Series Hurdle at Punchestown.

There is room at the top among the Irish hurdlers, at both around two miles and at longer trips, in other words. A couple of leading candidates to make the grade were novices in 2007/8. **Captain Cee Bee** and **Fiveforthree** gained two of Ireland's three Grade 1 successes at the Cheltenham Festival, the former at two miles in the Supreme Novices' Hurdle and the latter at two and a half

Captain Cee Bee (noseband) brings home a J.P. McManus one-two in the Supreme Novices' Hurdle

miles in the Baring Bingham Novices' Hurdle. Both were beaten subsequently—Captain Cee Bee running as if amiss at Aintree and Fiveforthree coming up short twice at Punchestown—but may still do better if persevered with over smaller obstacles. That does seem quite a big 'if', however, as both sets of connections are reportedly keen on a novice chase campaign in 2008/9.

Fiveforthree's handler, Willie Mullins, also trained the most highly-rated novice of the season in Ireland in **Cooldine**, winner of five consecutive races and one place behind Aitmatov in the World Series Hurdle at Punchestown. Cooldine is another likely to go over fences sooner rather than later, however. He is a good-topped, chasing type from a jumping family and promises to do very well in that sphere, especially as he was only seriously tested as a hurdler twice after mopping up a string of races in easy style.

The brightest hope from a hurdling point of view among last season's novices looks to be **Jered**, who won four of his seven races, notably the Dunboyne Castle Hotel & Spa Novices' Hurdle at Fairyhouse and the Champion Novices' Hurdle at Punchestown. Jered will have to do a lot better to mix it with the big boys in 2008/9—a two-length defeat of Made In Taipan and an eight-length defeat of Salford City respectively does not constitute better than useful form—but that seems entirely plausible given the manner of his successes. Those seem all the more meritorious when one considers that Jered's trainer, Noel Meade, was out of form for much of the second half of the campaign.

Jered looks a serious Champion Hurdle contender

A more obvious victim of the Meade stable's malaise was **Muirhead,** who won a bumper and his first two starts over hurdles, notably the Royal Bond Novices' Hurdle at Fairyhouse from Cork All Star, but who ran only once after the turn of the year, flopping behind Captain Cee Bee at Cheltenham when co-favourite. It would be no surprise were he to resume his progress in the months ahead and, as a five-year-old, he has time on his side before his attentions are turned to chasing.

One of Timeform's most highly-rated hurdlers with a 'p' (denoting the likelihood of improvement) was the Jessica Harrington-trained **Chasing Cars,** who ran Cooldine to three quarters of a length at Fairyhouse on what was just his fourth start over timber and first outside maiden company. Chasing Cars is another with the scope to take to fences when the time comes, but he could do well in staying hurdles first in view of how unexposed he is and the weakness of that division in Ireland.

Other significant Irish novice hurdle winners in 2007/8 included **Tranquil Sea,** who beat Fiveforthree at Punchestown and promises to stay three miles, **Forpadydeplasterer,** who had Tranquil Sea back in third when taking the Deloitte Novices' Hurdle at Leopardstown and who lost a shoe when fourth to Fiveforthree at Cheltenham, and **Venalmar** and **Trafford Lad,** first and second in the Slaney Novices' Hurdle at Naas and second and third to Fiveforthree at Cheltenham.

It is fair to say in the light of the above that there was not one dominant novice hurdler in Ireland during 2007/8, but that there was a fair bit of strength in depth and plenty of horses who promise much for the future, especially over fences.

In contrast, one gelding stood out in a weak division of Irish juvenile hurdlers, namely **Won In The Dark.** There was little to suggest that the son of Montjeu would make the grade over hurdles, as he was lacking in scope and a maiden on the Flat, not to mention the fact that his trainer Sabrina Harty had had just three career wins over jumps and one on the Flat at the start of the campaign. But make the grade he did, winning four of his eight starts, notably the Durkan New Homes Juvenile Hurdle at Leopardstown and the Champion Four Year Old Hurdle at Punchestown, and finishing third to Celestial Halo in the Triumph Hurdle at Cheltenham. He still has some way to go—at least a stone's improvement on Timeform ratings—to be a strong challenger for top open races, however, and life could be tough in his second season as a result.

Arguably a more interesting graduate from the four-year-old age group is **Hurricane Fly,** a useful miler on the Flat in France who made his debut shortly after the season's end and thus retains novice status for the 2008/9 campaign. The Willie Mullins-trained colt won well at Punchestown and Auteuil in May before finding only the home-trained Grivette too good for him in the Group 1 Prix Alain du Breil Hurdle at Auteuil in June. There should be more wins to come from him, especially when the emphasis is on speed, for all that the two Auteuil races were at nearly two and a half miles.

Mullins also trained the outstanding performer from a good crop of Irish bumper horses in **Cousin Vinny,** who not only remained undefeated in a campaign that took in the Champion Bumpers at Cheltenham and Punchestown but who recorded the highest Timeform rating for a bumper horse (134) since such ratings were introduced in the 1993/4 season. Mullins himself comments on Cousin Vinny in his interview in this publication, and many of the other leading bumper performers get a mention elsewhere.

Ireland continues to be a fine nursery for chasers, with Denman a particularly notable recent graduate from the pointing field, but the country has often failed to hold on to its potential stars. The cupboard was particularly bare at the top level in 2007/8, with Irish-trained chasers managing to win just one of the sixteen open Grade 1 chases in UK and Ireland, namely a weak Paddy Power Dial-A-Bet Chase at Leopardstown through **Mansony**.

Marginally best of the bunch was **Snowy Morning**, who failed to win over fences during the campaign and whose two best efforts were in finishing third in the Grand National at Aintree and second (beaten seven lengths by the Gold Cup third Neptune Collonges) in the Punchestown Guinness Gold Cup.

Snowy Morning had **Mossbank** seventeen lengths back in third at Punchestown, but that was not the latter's form. Mossbank had previously won the Munster National at Limerick and the Clonmel Oil Chase, and had been second to Denman in the Lexus Chase at Leopardstown and to Our Vic in the Ryanair Chase at Cheltenham. Unfortunately, it has been reported that the eight-year-old may miss the 2008/9 season altogether. **Our Ben** (killed in action) and **Beef Or Salmon** (retired) will also not be around, so there could be some easy pickings to be had in staying chases in the months ahead.

Mansony was challenged for top spot among the two-milers by **Nickname** (who managed just three runs and one win) and **Schindlers Hunt** (one win from seven starts), and it was the last-named who got closest of the Irish-trained horses to Master Minded in the Champion Chase at Cheltenham, being beaten thirty-six lengths into fourth.

With so much room at the top, domestically at least, the connections of some of the better Irish novice chasers of 2007/8 are entitled to feel optimistic. The best of them were probably just about **Big Zeb** and **Glencove Marina**, though the latter is another who's likely to miss 2008/9 through injury. Big Zeb, meanwhile, made up for arguably unfortunate defeats in the Dr P. J. Moriarty Novices' Chase at Leopardstown and the Powers Gold Cup at Fairyhouse with a convincing success in the Swordlestown Cup at Punchestown.

He looks like being best at two miles to two and a half miles, though it is possible he will get a bit further if ridden with more restraint than was sometimes the case in 2007/8, and one good thing was that his jumping held up well after a couple of falls early in his career.

Both of Thyne Again's two wins over fences as a novice came in graded company

Thyne Again won a Grade 1 (Arkle Perpetual Novices' Chase) and a Grade 2 in his native country but was manifestly inferior to a few among the two-mile to two-and-a-half-mile novice chasers, finishing a well-held fourth to Tidal Bay in the Arkle Chase at Cheltenham and four lengths second to Big Zeb at Punchestown. **Scotsirish** was favourite for the Arkle Perpetual but fell, and managed only seventh at Cheltenham, but is arguably a better prospect for 2008/9. His win under 11-10 in the betfair.com Novices' Handicap Chase at Punchestown was authoritative and represents smart form, and, as a son of Zaffaran, he has every prospect of being fully effective around three miles in due course.

It is very early days to speculate as to which horses from the Flat may make their marks over jumps in 2008/9, but a most interesting entry at the Listowel Festival in September was for the three-year-old **Lethal Weapon**. The useful but quirky son of Hawk Wing won easily at Navan and the Curragh for David Wachman in the first half of the 2008 Flat season (he is now with Christy Roche) and has the physical scope to take to jumping. There will not be many more talented recruits to hurdling in the months ahead.

Future Stars

Few systems can prove so consistently lucrative as highlighting talented trainers and jockeys before they are widely exposed to the racing public, so it is with plenty of hope, and no little expectation, that the quintet below are put forward as five to follow in 2008/9.

Jim Best

The ability to improve those they inherit from other stables is often used as the acid test of a trainer's skill, and nobody has made as favourable an impression

	NHF	Juveniles	Hurdlers	Chasers	All
Win prize money (£)					
2005/6			14,452	5,815	20,267
2006/7			20,754	3,253	24,007
2007/8			45,934	3,253	49,187
Cumulative			81,140	12,321	93,461
Winners-Horses					
2005/6			3-7	1-1	4-7
2006/7	0-2		5-10	1-1	6-13
2007/8		0-1	11-23	1-3	11-25
Cumulative	0-2	0-1	16-32	2-3	17-35
Wins-Runs					
2005/6			4-24	2-5	6-29
2006/7	0-2		7-27	1-5	8-34
2007/8		0-1	17-96	1-11	18-108
Cumulative	0-2	0-1	28-147	4-21	32-171
Strike Rate (%)					
2005/6			17	40	21
2006/7	0		26	20	24
2007/8		0	18	9	17
Cumulative	0	0	19	19	19
Profit / Loss (£1)					
2005/6			5.00	11.00	16.00
2006/7	-2.00		16.95	.50	15.45
2007/8		-1.00	-2.79	-7.50	-11.29
Cumulative	-2.00	-1.00	19.16	4.00	20.16
Median Rating					
2005/6			96	76	96
2006/7	–		91	85	88
2007/8		76	99	85	93
Cumulative	–	76	95	85	91

on that score in the last year or so as Jim Best, aided in his operation by brother and fellow former amateur rider, Tom. Their knack at getting the maximum out of their inmates has extended to the Flat, too, in recent times, but it is as a National Hunt yard that they are best known and the likes of Dundridge Native, Wotchalike and Lady Pilot, horses all of limited ability with whom Best has wrought improvement, have flown the flag for the stable. Hopefully, the standard in Best's yard will improve, as it deserves to, as he certainly has the ability and desire to more than hold his own at a higher level.

Trainer's view: Tom and I went to over sixty yards before we set up and liked the way Paul Nicholls did things. Along with that and what we learned from others, we've tried to adapt our own training regime. We were really pleased with how things went last season, and we're looking forward to another good one having jumped up another level with the type of horse we've bought.

Horse To Follow: **Hello Moscow**—He won point-to-points and used to be with Michael Hourigan. He'll go hurdling this season, or maybe even start in a bumper as he was just touched off in one in Ireland. He looks a good horse to follow.

Tim Vaughan

Peter Bowen and Evan Williams once stood out as the prominent trainers in Wales, but Keith Goldsworthy and Tim Vaughan have made quite an impression in trying to match them in recent times and the last-named in particular appeals as a man to keep on side in 2008/9. In truth, it was a tough choice between the pair, and there'd be worse advice than to follow both, but the momentum certainly seems to be with Vaughan, who, at the time of writing, has already amassed twenty winners over jumps since May (had fourteen in all last season) at an impressive strike rate of almost 20%. Vaughan is well equipped to add plenty more to that haul with the size of his string, as well as his reputation, seemingly growing all the while.

Trainer's view: I had fourteen horses in March and we've progressed and got two yards now with fifty-two in one and twenty in another. The hope is this year to keep it going through the winter which we haven't managed to do before, and I hope we've got the ammunition now to compete.

Horse To Follow: **Abou Ben**—He's had only one run in a bumper. It was a weak race, but he did it comfortably and he's a two-and-a-half-mile hurdler in

	NHF	Juveniles	Hurdlers	Chasers	All
Win prize money (£)					
2005/6				6,496	6,496
2006/7				2,928	2,928
2007/8	3,802		33,052	9,108	45,962
Cumulative	3,802		33,052	18,532	55,386
Winners-Horses					
2005/6			0-5	1-1	1-5
2006/7	0-2	0-3	0-7	1-5	1-14
2007/8	1-6		6-12	1-6	7-21
Cumulative	1-7	0-3	6-22	3-11	9-35
Wins-Runs					
2005/6			0-8	1-2	1-10
2006/7	0-3	0-10	0-15	1-6	1-34
2007/8	2-11		10-35	2-14	14-60
Cumulative	2-14	0-10	10-58	4-22	16-104
Strike Rate (%)					
2005/6			0	50	10
2006/7	0	0	0	17	3
2007/8	18		29	14	23
Cumulative	14		17	18	15
Profit / Loss (£1)					
2005/6			-8.00	5.50	-2.50
2006/7	-3.00	-10.00	-15.00	1.00	-27.00
2007/8	18.50		16.25	-2.00	32.75
Cumulative	15.50	-10.00	-6.75	4.50	3.25
Median Rating					
2005/6			–	103	–
2006/7	69	–	79	81	65
2007/8	70		90	94	90
Cumulative	69	–	76	96	75

the longer term. He's schooled very well and he'll have one more outing in a bumper before he goes hurdling.

Liam Corcoran

Less heralded than even Best and Vaughan is Liam Corcoran who, like that pair and so many others who've done well in the training ranks, made his name originally as a jumps jockey. Admittedly, Corcoran's strike rate isn't on a par with that pair, or for that matter anywhere near the best in the country, but he's had some pretty limited material on his hands—when getting the right ammunition he can do his job as well as anybody. For instance, note the work he's done so far this season with Advancement, a cheap purchase from Richard Fahey's stable, who's won three times over hurdles and been placed in a valuable handicap at Market Rasen, and Magical Legend, who progressed to finish second in a listed mares handicap hurdle at Cheltenham last season.

Trainer's view: We've had a very good start this season. It was frustrating last year as we had a lot of young horses who weren't ready, but we did the right thing giving them time and they've come back bigger and stronger. We've got twenty-nine in and we hope to keep the show on the road and get more winners.

Horse To Follow: Romance Dance—She was second to Dancingwithbubbles at Folkestone and to one of Oliver Sherwood's at Chepstow, and was then

	NHF	Juveniles	Hurdlers	Chasers	All
Win prize money (£)					
2005/6	1,869		20,481		22,350
2006/7			13,495	5,530	19,025
2007/8			21,207	3,578	24,785
Cumulative	1,869		55,183	9,108	66,160
Winners-Horses					
2005/6	1-3	0-3	3-10	0-4	3-16
2006/7	0-3	0-3	4-19	1-4	5-26
2007/8	0-5	0-3	5-22	1-3	6-30
Cumulative	1-10	0-9	10-39	2-11	12-57
Wins-Runs					
2005/6	1-4	0-8	3-26	0-6	4-44
2006/7	0-7	0-12	5-49	1-5	6-73
2007/8	0-7	0-5	7-69	1-8	8-89
Cumulative	1-18	0-25	15-144	2-19	18-206
Strike Rate (%)					
2005/6	25	0	12	0	9
2006/7	0	0	10	20	8
2007/8	0	0	10	13	9
Cumulative	6	0	10	11	9
Profit / Loss (£1)					
2005/6	7.00	-8.00	38.50	-6.00	31.50
2006/7	-7.00	-12.00	-4.37	2.00	-21.37
2007/8	-7.00	-5.00	-28.09	5.00	-35.09
Cumulative	-7.00	-25.00	6.04	1.00	-24.96
Median Rating					
2005/6	–	81	67	–	67
2006/7	89	–	88	94	88
2007/8	–	–	–	94	–
Cumulative	81	–	77	88	77

beaten seven lengths in the mares listed race at Aintree. She's not really a bumper horse as she wants two and a half miles and we'll hopefully contest the mares only races. She jumps well, too.

Aidan Coleman

His claim might have been reduced to 3 lb now, but there's no doubt Aidan Coleman is going to make it as a fully-fledged jockey in time and he'll remain a rider to follow even when his allowance has gone completely. The case for Coleman is simple—he's a stylish, sensible rider, who's excellent tactically, and, in contrast to some of even the top jockeys who've burst through in recent times, he gets the best out of his mounts without the call for brute strength alone. All in all, Coleman's future is as bright as any rider's around, and it can only help that he's retained by Venetia Williams, the trainer who played such an important role in the development of Sam Thomas, a jockey in a similar mould.

Stan (far side) gives the highly promising Aidan Coleman a first win at Aintree

Jockey's view: I've been delighted so far, things have been going great, and a couple more big winners this season would be nice. I still ride out at Venetia's most mornings, and she's got a good history with jockeys. If this goes as well as last season I won't have a claim and we'll have to see how things go then.

Horse To Follow: Flintoff—I rode him only three times last season and he was thereabouts on each occasion. He ran well in the Irish National, Scottish National and a valuable race at Haydock and hopefully he can win one.

Charlie Huxley

Whilst plain old ability is obviously of most importance in a young jockey's make-up, the temperament to handle the big occasion is another must, and no other amateur rider showcased that as well as Charlie Huxley last season. Huxley first had rides outside of points in 2005, but his stock rightly rose last season as he took the eye several times, and it was no surprise Alan King entrusted Huxley with the mount on Old Benny in the National Hunt Chase at Cheltenham. It was Huxley's first ride at the Festival, but it would have been hard to tell as he was faultless from start to finish in Old Benny's win, just as he was when steering Iris de Balme to a shock success in the Scottish National the following month. Still able to claim 7 lb, Huxley turned professional soon after the latter success, and he'll be bang there in the race to be champion conditional in 2008/9.

Jockey's view: I had a brilliant season and was lucky enough to ride a winner at Cheltenham and in the Scottish National. I owe plenty to my sponsor Lee Power and agent Chris Broad, while I've had a lot of support from Alan King and I've got a great relationship with Sean Curran, too. I don't like to set targets, but I'd hope to ride forty winners this season.

Horse To Follow: Iris de Balme—He's still a maiden over hurdles, but he's a possible for the Welsh and Aintree Nationals—his defeat at Sandown was half my fault and I felt he was still improving then.

Handicappers' Corner

Breakwater House (Timeform Rating 85p) has the potential to be well handicapped from a mark of 95 when stepped up to a trip more in line with his pedigree. The six-year-old had fairly useful novice chaser Star Player back in third when making a successful racecourse debut in a bumper at Newcastle in January 2007, and he's looked to face an inadequate test of stamina on all four outings over hurdles since returning from a twelve-month absence. His unraced dam was out of a half-sister to the 1996 Cheltenham Gold Cup winner Imperial Call, and Breakwater House remains likely to be of interest in handicaps in the North when stepped up to two and a half miles and more.
Miss Lucinda Russell

High Jack (Timeform Rating 97+, c97+), who represents the same owner/trainer as his half-brother and one of the members of the fifty Bible Lord, came extremely close to making the list himself. Having shaped with promise in a stronger race on his only previous start in a handicap hurdle, he broke his duck at the tenth attempt when landing a similar event for conditional riders at Towcester in April, responding generously to wear down Once at the last. The manner of his success suggests that he'll be of similar interest in that sphere this season from a mark 6 lb higher. However, given both his breeding and his stature High Jack makes even more appeal for handicaps over the larger obstacles from a mark of just 87. He shaped well when making his chasing debut in a two-mile handicap at Hereford in December, jumping soundly by and large and in third when falling at the last. Admittedly, he failed to build on that in similar events afterwards, but being a brother to the 2005 Aintree Fox Hunters' runner-up Caught At Dawn and a half-brother to another fairly useful chaser Kew Jumper, High Jack will almost certainly be seen to better effect granted a stiffer test of stamina. It's difficult not to see him winning races over fences in the coming months.
Andrew Turnell

Krackatara (Timeform Rating 130p) caught the eye in no uncertain terms when finishing just outside the frame in a Chepstow novice on his second start over hurdles. He was subsequently found to have suffered a breathing problem, but clearly it wasn't a serious one as nine days later he returned to the course for a maiden and justified strong support. Krackatara once more travelled noticeably strongly, and he asserted in good style from four out to beat Tank Top by six lengths despite going markedly left at the last. The son of Kayf Tara would have followed up at Exeter on his handicap debut just over a month later but for tipping up at the last, when six lengths ahead of eventual winner Or Bleu. Krackatara will start the season off a mark just 5 lb higher than at Exeter, and it's one he should gain compensation from. *Mrs S Gardner*

Letalus (Timeform Rating 96, c125+) is probably not the most straightforward of performers, but there is no doubt that he is a chaser on the up, one whose style of racing could keep him ahead of the handicapper for a little while yet. Things really clicked for this lightly-raced seven-year-old when he was reunited with Paul Maloney, winning at Wincanton and Warwick on his last two starts. Exaggerated waiting tactics were adopted on each occasion, and on the latter course, where he travelled best and also jumped well, Letalus was coaxed along to lead virtually on the line after being switched inside on the run-in. He reportedly received a knock soon after and he missed the remainder of the season, but he will be one for punters to keep on the right side when he returns to action, hopefully after Christmas. *Carl Llewellyn*

Noir Et Vert (Timeform Rating c129) could put the bank balances of those who follow him this season well into the former. His trainer Ferdy Murphy teamed up to good effect with Richard Harding at Cheltenham in 2006, the combination landing both the National Hunt Chase and the Kim Muir, and he again had the services of the Irish amateur when Noir Et Vert made a belated seasonal return in the latter contest at last season's Festival. The Plantation Stud-owned gelding had been highly progressive over fences in 2006/7, and on his final start had been beaten only a short head in a valuable handicap at Punchestown. At Cheltenham he travelled better than any other runner in the race bar the winner, High Chimes, until his long absence seemed to tell from three out, eventually fading into fourth. On the back of that display and with drying conditions looking to suit him more than the majority of the field, Noir Et Vert was the subject of a gamble for the Scottish National. He failed to justify the promise of his comeback run, but it is easy to overlook his performance at Ayr, where he raced from almost a stone out of the weights and was ridden by an inexperienced claimer, a mistake at the twentieth also not helping his cause. Noir Et Vert remains likely to prove suited by very long distances and a mark of 130 could see him as a live candidate for top honours in one of the big staying handicaps, with the Grand National itself not out of the question later on. *Ferdy Murphy*

The Great Alfie (Timeform Rating 117p) wouldn't be one of the better-known names to race from the Nigel Twiston-Davies stable in 2007/8, but from what he achieved in his first season there's every reason to believe he'll be adding significantly to his one victory to date. That success came at Perth on his handicap debut. Stepped up markedly in trip, The Great Alfie began to fulfil the promise he'd shown in a couple of bumpers, battling on well to beat My Arch by a length and a quarter and give his trainer the first of his four winners on the card. An 8-lb rise doesn't seem at all harsh and is unlikely to prevent The Great Alfie winning again over hurdles when he returns, though it's surely over fences that his future lies, given his imposing build and his pedigree—he's from the family of the useful staying chaser Dakyns Boy. *N Twiston-Davies*

The Bumper Scene

Cousin Vinny—we've not seen one of his like in bumpers before

The greatest bumper performer since Timeform first published comprehensive figures for such races in 1993/4. That was the accolade bestowed on **Cousin Vinny** (F134) after he romped to victory in the Paddy Power Champion INH Flat race at Punchestown, in so doing becoming the first to complete the Cheltenham-Punchestown double since the then-Festival bumper was introduced at Cheltenham in 1992. Cousin Vinny had already produced a smart performance to land the Weatherbys Champion Bumper at Cheltenham in decisive fashion from **Corskeagh Royale** (F122) and **Zaarito** (F121), Irish-trained horses filling all bar one of the first seven placings, but his one at Punchestown was of a higher standard still. Again ridden by trainer Willie Mullins' son Patrick, who had also been in the saddle at Cheltenham where he'd been up against mainly professional jockeys yet was unable to claim, Cousin Vinny ran even further away from his field this time, crossing the line fully ten lengths clear of **Endless Intrigue** (F116) with **Academy Sir Harry** (F119) a further two and a half lengths back in third, Corskeagh Royale finishing in the frame again but beaten a good deal further than had been the case at Cheltenham. Willie Mullins has built up a tremendous record in the Champion Bumper at Cheltenham in the last dozen or so years, winning it on no less than six occasions, including with Florida Pearl and Alexander Banquet, who both went on to be top-class staying chasers, and Missed That, a dual Grade 1 winner over fences before suffering a fatal injury at home. There are good reasons for believing Cousin Vinny will make a big impact over jumps, too. Lengthy and rather unfurnished at present, he comes from the Trix family, best known for its staying chasers, 1990 Scottish National winner Four Trix among them, though he is related to speedier types in Hidebound, a useful but fragile two-mile hurdler, and fairly useful two-mile hurdler Hot Zone.

Of those who have suffered at the hands of Cousin Vinny, Corskeagh Royale won twice by a wide margin before going to Cheltenham, including in a Grade 2 event at Navan, though his tendency to swish his tail under pressure is somewhat disconcerting; Zaarito, who went off favourite but didn't get a clear run at Cheltenham, went one better than Corskeagh Royale in winning his first three starts and is from the family of the very smart staying chaser Young Kenny, though he is distinctly lacking in scope himself; dual-winner Endless Intrigue is related to good horses his trainer Dermot Weld has had in the past, namely 2000 Guineas winner Refuse To Bend and Melbourne Cup winner Media Puzzle, and is likely to have a bit more speed than most bumper horses that go jumping; Fairyhouse winner Academy Sir Harry doesn't have the pedigree of an obvious jumper, either, though shapes as if he will stay at least two and a half miles and should still make a useful-or-better novice hurdler, and **Apt Approach** (F120), who went off the shortest price of Mullins' four runners in the Champion Bumper at Cheltenham after an impressive win at Gowran, didn't build on that run but can still be expected to make his mark as a jumper (fell at the last when clear in a point) judged on looks and pedigree, his unraced dam a half-sister to Irish Grand National winner Feathered Gale.

Outside the top races, there was the usual plethora of promising performances from once/twice-raced sorts in bumpers in Ireland last season. Among those likely to make even more of a name for themselves over jumps are **Jaffonnien** (F114p), who won at Leopardstown on his debut with something in hand, and **Pandorama** (F110p), a stoutly-bred point winner who scored by a wide margin at Fairyhouse. **Astute Approach** (F110p) and **Smoking Aces** (F108p), winners at Fairyhouse and Thurles respectively, also have plenty to recommend them on breeding, the latter a half-brother to useful chaser Roll Along from the family of Cheltenham Gold Cup winner Charter Party. In addition, a lot more should be heard of **Paul Kristian** (F107p) judged on the promise shown by the point winner in a bumper at Gowran and a maiden hurdle at Limerick, his jockey in the latter event hit with a hefty ban for making insufficient effort. It should also pay to make a note of the well-bred **Uimhiraceathair** (F116), who beat Academy Sir Harry impressively at Navan and again looked a stayer when accounting for **Total Excitement** (F114) in a useful event at the Curragh in early-May.

Unlike the Cheltenham and Punchestown races, the championship event at Aintree is only a Grade 2 but the 2008 running looks of a higher standard than any of the last five renewals, with the field strung out at the end of a race which provided a really good test under the conditions. It was a triumph for northern-based trainers, who were responsible for six of the first seven home, notably **Honest John** (F119), who'd run just once before and was one of only three maidens in the field. It wasn't as if he didn't come in for support, however, and he was going away at the line, his victory enough to help persuade Graham Wylie to pay £115,000 for his Doncaster conqueror **Doeslessthanme** (F112p), who'd also won at Musselburgh on his only other outing for Clive Mulhall. If anything, Aintree runner-up **Touch of Irish** (F118) has still more potential as a jumper than Honest John given his impressive physique and the fact he clearly possesses a lot of speed for one bred as he is—by Kayf Tara out of a winning pointer. He'd won both his previous starts and ran close to his best at Punchestown despite finishing just out of the frame. The next four home at Aintree were also unbeaten going into the race, and though **Cape Tribulation** (F116) and Haydock winner **Cloudy Times** (F113) are chiefly bred for the Flat both should nevertheless make their mark in novice hurdles this season. That said, **Copper Bleu** (F111) promises to do even better; a tall gelding with scope and a half-brother to his connections' fairly useful hurdler/chaser Presenting Copper, he'd won a point and a bumper (for Donal Coffey) in Ireland before being snapped up for £155,000 at the Cheltenham January Sales and, along with **Cockney Trucker** (F112) who was the second British-trained runner across the line in the Champion Bumper at Cheltenham, forms part of a fine team of novice hurdlers at Philip Hobbs's disposal this season.

Not that Hobbs's squad will have quite the strength in depth of that of Champion Trainer Paul Nicholls, whose batch of useful novice hurdle prospects was bolstered still further by the arrival of **Charity Lane** (F115), who was bought for Andy Stewart for £200,000 at the Doncaster May Sales after he'd won two bumpers then not been at all discredited under less testing conditions when sixth to Honest John at Aintree. His long-term future lies over fences but he should still be able to pick up at least a couple of races over hurdles when his stamina is brought into play. Along with the exciting **Conflictofinterest** (F110p), the likes of **Mahonia** (F111), who beat subsequent useful hurdle winner The Jazz Musician at Chepstow before finishing in mid-division in the Champion Bumper at Cheltenham, and **Fistral Beach** (F111p), who created a really favourable impression when beating stable-companion Our Bomber Harris at Newton Abbot, can't help but win races over hurdles providing they stay clear of injury. That comment also applies to **The Nightingale** (F109), who having won well at Wincanton on his debut chased home Mad Max in a Grade 2 contest at Newbury. There was no disgrace at all in that, given that **Mad Max** (F120) ended up the highest-rated British-trained bumper horse of 2007/8 (ignoring those who ran in the rearranged early-season event at Aintree) despite not running in any of the championship events. That was by design, as he's so big (trainer Nicky Henderson believes he's the biggest racehorse he's ever seen) that it was considered best to put him away with his jumping career in mind. Distances in excess of two miles are likely to suit Mad Max judged on pedigree (by Kayf Tara out of a useful staying chaser) and the way he saw out the race at Newbury.

A couple of last season's leading bumper horses sure to need further than the minimum trip over hurdles are **Voice of Reason** (F119) and **Blencathra Bay** (F116), the two having finished clear of subsequent Champion Bumper fourth **Shoreacres** (F116) in a stamina-sapping listed event at Warwick in January. The first-named had won at Folkestone first time out and, though he wasn't seen out again after Warwick, he's back cantering and likely to be ready to run by the end of October. Blencathra Bay is very much a chasing sort in appearance and, whilst he was unable to cope with the greater test of speed he faced on his final start at Aintree, there are more races to be won with him over longer distances.

So far as the number of individual winners in bumpers last season is concerned Alan King's record was outstanding. No fewer than twenty of the yard's horses were successful in that division (four more than Paul Nicholls and David Pipe combined), winning twenty-six times between them, with **Bakbenscher** (F115) and **Shalone** (F115+) both doing enough to warrant their inclusion in the fifty and **Dancingwithbubbles** (F112) ending up the season's highest-rated British-trained mare in bumpers despite being pipped by the four-year-old Dayia in a listed event at Sandown. The best performance put up by a mare in bumpers in Ireland came courtesy of **Grancore Girl** (F114), a sister to useful staying hurdler Black Harry who won on bad ground at Clonmel and Limerick in March. The only horse to beat Shalone in that one's three starts was another who finds himself in the main part of this publication, the rangy **Diamond Harry** (F116) who has earned connections over £64,000 by virtue of winning the same valuable sales race at Newbury twelve months apart.

Cheltenham Ante-Post Betting

'A mug's game' or 'the only way to bet on big races'? Opinion is certainly divided on ante-post betting, with critics of the practice arguing that the risks involved far outweigh the bigger odds that the early markets invariably offer. The biggest risk, of course, is that ante-post punters lose their cash in the event of backing a non-runner. This was very relevant in the ante-post markets drawn up last autumn for the big novice events at the Cheltenham Festival, with none of the fifteen horses quoted for the Baring Bingham Novices' Hurdle actually making the line-up six months later. The equivalent lists for the Supreme Novices' Hurdle and Triumph Hurdle yielded just one runner apiece, seventh-placed Cork All Star (12/1 ante-post, but 17/2 on the day) in the former and ninth-placed Temlett (20/1 joint favourite in late-September, but 100/1 come March) in the latter. Clearly, there will be plenty of losing ante-post bets already safely in the bookmakers' coffers before the 2009 Festival even gets underway, particularly as one High Street firm has again been offering prices for six races at the meeting since the summer. However, it isn't all doom and gloom for ante-post punters. Indeed, it is very doubtful those shrewdies who took three-figure prices about Sublimity and Kauto Star in early-2006/7 had any complaints when that duo landed the Champion Hurdle and Cheltenham Gold Cup respectively later in the season. The advent of the betting exchanges has unquestionably helped punters manage their ante-post liabilities a good deal better. If an ante-post selection is cut markedly in price over the winter, punters now have the option of covering his or her original stake by laying that horse off at much shorter odds. In addition, anyone who lays one of the leading ante-post fancies has the option to back it at longer odds should that selection drift in price over the winter—Champion Hurdle winner Katchit went off 10/1 on the day, having been 4/1 prior to two defeats in the winter.

The reigning champions head the ante-post markets for all four of Cheltenham's showpiece races—the Champion Hurdle, the Queen Mother Champion Chase, the World Hurdle and the Cheltenham Gold Cup—though the statistics aren't really stacked in that quartet's favour. Best Mate is the only multiple Cheltenham Gold Cup winner during the last thirty-seven years, whilst Viking Flagship in 1995 was the last back-to-back winner of the Champion Chase (though Moscow Flyer did regain the crown in the interim). Paul Nicholls appears to hold the key to both races at present, especially in the Cheltenham Gold Cup, having saddled the first three home last March with Denman, Kauto

Star and Neptune Collonges. That trio, understandably, head the ante-post market at present, whilst the likes of Big Buck's, Star de Mohaison and Gungadu are other Gold Cup contenders from the stable also quoted in those lists. The 2007 winner Kauto Star almost certainly wasn't at his very best in the latest Gold Cup, so the 5/1 currently on offer about him clearly appeals as the value bet against Denman's best price of just 11/8, especially with concerns over the latter's well-being. There doesn't appear to be much value on offer elsewhere in this ante-post market, however, particularly as there are doubts about the participation of unexposed types such as Tidal Bay (not certain to be campaigned at staying trips) and Glencove Marina (may miss 2008/9 due to injury), so punters would be advised to keep their powder dry for the time being.

By contrast, there could be some each-way value around in the two-mile championship for chasers. Master Minded, understandably, is a firm favourite on the back of his runaway success in the latest renewal of the Queen Mother Champion Chase and could well dominate this division for some time to come, particularly as there is a good chance his two closest rivals in the ante-post market, Tidal Bay and Voy Por Ustedes, will run in other races at the Festival. Master Minded's stable-companion Twist Magic clearly didn't give his running in the latest Champion Chase, and given that he notched up two Grade 1 wins away from Cheltenham in 2007/8 he will no doubt have some supporters at around 16/1. However, Nicholls is responsible for two other possible runners in **Takeroc** (16/1) and **Andreas** (33/1), both of whom appeal as better ante-post alternatives at present. Takeroc joined the stable fairly late in 2007/8 but wasted little time in announcing himself as a very exciting prospect, following his smooth win at Sandown in March with an excellent second to Tidal Bay in the Grade 1 Maghull Novices' Chase at Aintree. Although he failed to justify favouritism when reverted to smaller obstacles for the Scottish Champion Hurdle at Ayr on his final start, Takeroc still enhanced his reputation with second place that day and it certainly wouldn't be a surprise if he overtook Twist Magic in the pecking order at Manor Farm Stables this winter. Unlike the names already mentioned, Andreas has plied his trade almost exclusively in handicap company since graduating from the novice ranks, including a win in the 2007 Grand Annual at Cheltenham (also good fourth in 2008 under top weight). A strong-travelling sort, Andreas was most impressive when upped in class for his final outing of last season, winning the Celebration Chase at Sandown by nine lengths. Given he's now on a BHA mark of 162, it wouldn't be a surprise if connections opted to campaign Andreas in graded company this winter and, as Nicholls clearly isn't adverse to being multi-handed in the big races, he could

Andreas appeals as a lively outsider for the Queen Mother Champion Chase

develop into a live outsider. Clearly, the odds for both Takeroc and Andreas will look very big should loss of form and/or injury befall Master Minded, whilst they still make appeal even if the favourite rules the roost as expected—Master Minded could scare off potential rivals, which may result in ante-post bets (with each-way terms covering the first three home) being settled in a race with less than eight runners on the day.

One has to go back to 1974 for the last Champion Hurdle field of less than eight runners and it's most unlikely that trend will be broken in 2009 if the ante-post markets are anything to go by—this is the most open betting heat of the Festival's four top championship races at present, with Katchit (best price 6/1) and Binocular (7/1) vying for favouritism. Reigning champion Katchit can boast a record of ten wins and three placed efforts from thirteen starts over hurdles, which illustrates that there is far more to his repertoire than simply his renowned toughness. This hugely likeable gelding seems sure to be in the mix again in 2009, but he doesn't appeal as great value at current odds, particularly as the bare form of his win last March isn't anything special compared to past winners of hurdling's blue riband event. Indeed, **Sizing Europe** might have flopped at Cheltenham when a short-priced favourite (went amiss when holding every chance two out), but his win in the Irish Champion Hurdle earlier in the season was arguably the best two-mile performance of 2007/8 and he makes more appeal at current odds of 10/1, particularly as connections have shelved plans to go chasing with him for another season. That said, at least Katchit (together with third-placed Punjabi) exploded the myth about five-year-olds being best avoided in the Champion Hurdle due to their perceived bad record in the race. That age group seems set to be well represented in 2009, as last season's leading juveniles looked an above-average crop. Chief amongst them was the J. P. McManus-owned Binocular, who comprehensively defeated Triumph Hurdle winner Celestial Halo at Aintree, whilst his earlier close second to Captain Cee Bee (set to go chasing in 2008/9) in the Supreme Novices' Hurdle came in a race which was run in a quicker time than the Champion Hurdle later on the same card. McManus looks to hold a strong hand, as the Noel Meade-trained **Jered** impressed as a top-notch prospect when completing a hat-trick in smooth fashion in the Grade 1 Champion Novices' Hurdle at Punchestown in April. Tony McCoy will have a difficult job in choosing between the pair but, given that the Irish gelding is currently double the odds of Binocular, it is a straightforward task for ante-post punters, and 14/1 about Jered could well look very big come next March should conditions place the emphasis on speed. Similar comments apply to Punjabi (16/1), whose third place in last season's Champion Hurdle was all the more creditable when one considers things didn't go his way. Punjabi confirmed Cheltenham placings with Sublimity on his only subsequent outing at Punchestown, a victory which has possibly been underestimated due to a fine tactical ride by Barry Geraghty, who'll keep the ride following his link-up with Nicky Henderson this season. Although he trails Katchit three-nil in their head-to-head meetings, Punjabi is the sort with which Henderson traditionally excels and he has been better than ever on the Flat in 2008.

Paul Nicholls hasn't been anything like the dominant force he has over fences when it comes to the top hurdlers, having saddled just two runners in the Champion Hurdle and only one in the World Hurdle—all three finished unplaced. The Champion Trainer is reportedly keen to address this discrepancy in 2008/9, citing his two leading juveniles from last season, Pierrot Lunaire and Celestial Halo, plus the ex-South African gelding Rippling Ring, as possibles for the two-mile event. However, the stable's World Hurdle contender **Elusive Dream** (14/1) appears to hold a better chance at present, particularly as three-times winner Inglis Drever could prove vulnerable to up-and-coming rivals in 2008/9, which is reputedly due to be his final campaign. Elusive Dream was of a similar standard to Inglis Drever on the Flat—when they were both trained by Sir Mark Prescott—and has also taken very well to hurdling despite a fairly late start (he was forced to sit out 2006/7 due to an 'allergic reaction'). He was one of the leading novices of 2007/8, when his five wins included a defeat of Whiteoak and Franchoek in the Grade 2 Mersey Novices' at Aintree, and the step up to three miles is unlikely to pose a problem. However, a better alternative could well be one of his Aintree victims, **Franchoek**, who makes plenty of appeal at current odds of 33/1. This Alan King-trained gelding might have had to settle for minor honours at the major spring festivals but he was still very much one of last season's leading juveniles (four wins) and may yet do better when his stamina is tested more fully. Indeed, that Aintree third is his only attempt at around two and a half miles to date and he wasn't seen to best advantage, getting trapped behind fading rivals as Elusive Dream got first run before keeping on well. Franchoek should stay three miles and has good prospects of emulating his stable-companion Blazing Bailey (7/1), a similarly tough gelding who progressed into a high-class stayer after finishing placed in the Triumph Hurdle as a juvenile.

As for the other markets currently on offer for Cheltenham Festival races, punters are reminded about the numerous non-runners from the corresponding ante-post lists last autumn. For the record, the names that catch the eye at this stage are Captain Cee Bee (12/1) in the Arkle and both Forpadydeplaster (16/1) and Beshabar (25/1) in the Royal & SunAlliance Chase, but those odds aren't sufficiently big enough to be playing at, particularly as none of that trio has even jumped a fence in public yet. Such a concern isn't an issue for those featured in the ante-post market for National Hunt racing's biggest betting race, the Grand National, with last season's first three Comply Or Die, King Johns Castle and Snowy Morning all vying for favouritism in those lists that don't feature Denman—the Gold Cup winner is likely to tackle Aintree's famous fences at some stage but, according to connections, it won't be in 2009. This is another race, however, where many contenders will have fallen by the wayside by next April, so any ante-post interest should be small and at sizeable odds. With that in mind, anyone wishing to get involved at this stage could do a lot worse than An Accordion and Butler's Cabin, both of whom have valuable staying handicap wins on their CV.

MAIN RECOMMENDATIONS

Queen Mother Champion Chase **Takeroc (16/1) & Andreas (33/1)**

Champion Hurdle **Jered (14/1) & Sizing Europe (10/1)**

World Hurdle **Franchoek (33/1) & Elusive Dream (14/1)**

Selected Big Races from Cheltenham In Perspective

The daily reports of Timeform's representatives on the course form the basis of *Timeform Perspective*. Their observations, supplemented by those of Timeform's handicappers and comment writers, make *Timeform Perspective* thoroughly informative. Here are some key races from last spring's major Festival meetings in Britain chosen from the Timeform Form-Book.

CHELTENHAM Tue, Mar 11

4045 Anglo Irish Bank Supreme Nov Hdle (Gr 1) (1) 2m110y (8)
(4yo+) £68,424

```
2141°  CAPTAIN CEE BEE (IRE) EPHarty,Ireland 7-11-7            1
       RobertThornton ..................................... 11 17/2
3711°  BINOCULAR (FR) NJHenderson 4-10-13 APMcCoy........ 8/1cf  2  2
2624²  SNAP TIE (IRE) PJHobbs 6-11-7 RichardJohnson....... 20/1  4½  3
3719²  Kalahari King (FR) FerdyMurphy 7-11-7 TonyDobbin .... 40/1  5  4
3362°  Rippling Ring (SAF) PFNicholls 5-11-7 RWalsh....... 8 10/1  2¼  5
3484   Blue Bajan (IRE) AndrewTurnell 6-11-7 TomScudamore ....  33/1  1½  6
3515²  Cork All Star (IRE) MrsJHarrington,Ireland 6-11-7 BJGeraghty.. 10 17/2  1  7
3515³  Tranquil Sea (IRE) EJO'Grady,Ireland 6-11-7 AJMcNamara ... 20 18/1  4  8
3039²  Deep Purple EvanWilliams 7-11-7 PaulMoloney ...... 20 16/1  ¾  9
3251⁴  Khyber Kim NJHenderson 7-11-7 MickFitzgerald ...... 8 17/2  2¼ 10
3708°  Pigeon Island NATwiston-Davies 5-11-7 PJBrennan ... 9 8/1cf  17 11
2450°  Muirhead (IRE) NMeade,Ireland 5-11-7 PCarberry ...... 8/1cf  6 12
3708⁴  Numide (FR) GLMoore 5-11-7 (t) JamieMoore ...... 33/1  10 13
3274⁴  The Gloves Are Off (IRE) MFMorris,Ireland 5-11-7 DNRussell ... 33/1  22 14
3364°  Sentry Duty (FR) NJHenderson 6-11-7 AndrewTinkler ...... 11/1  4½ 15
3398⁵  Sophocles JamesLeavy,Ireland 5-11-7 DJCasey ...... 100/1  6 17
3783°  Quartano (GER) CarlLlewellyn 5-11-7 NoelFehily ...... 100/1  6 17
3498²  Calgary Bay (IRE) MissHCKnight 5-11-7 TimmyMurphy ...... 40/1  9 18
3629⁴  Lemon Silk (IRE) KJBurke 4-10-13 PCO'Neill ...... 150/1  1¾ 19
1801²  Norther Bay (FR) EoinGriffin,Ireland 5-11-7 TomDoyle ..... 150/1  pu
3480°  Pasco (SWI) PFNicholls 5-11-7 SamThomas ...... 16/1  pu
3719⁴  Striking Article (IRE) JHowardJohnson 6-11-7 DenisO'Regan .... 100/1  pu
```

2.00race Mr John P. McManus 22ran 4m06.56

An amazingly open renewal of the top race of the season for 2m novice hurdlers, with none having shown the form required to win an average recent running but plenty having the potential to progress, the field a good mix of good ex-Flat horses and those from a bumper background, one of each group fighting out the finish; a heavy shower shortly before racing ensured softer ground than customary in recent years for the opening day of the Festival and conditions played their part in the pace of this, the overall tempo little more than fair, the race gradually taking shape once the early clear leader was headed at the fifth. **Captain Cee Bee** belied doubts about his effectiveness on soft ground, putting up a smart effort and a game one too, pushed along at the fifth and not going so well as quite a few down the hill but staying on to challenge after 2 out and lead in the last 100 yds; he may well have more to offer as a hurdler, though also has the physique to make a chaser and could well be back as a leading Arkle candidate in 2009, if connections choose that route. **Binocular** was sweating and on his toes beforehand but once again that didn't hinder his performance, as he improved again from Kempton, going well when leading after 2 out but unable to stay on quite so stoutly as the winner after the last; he probably has further improvement in him, perhaps when facing more of a test of speed, so would certainly be an interesting runner in the Anniversary Hurdle; he was running here in preference to the Triumph, presumably as the owner has a strong candidate for that, even though the trainer has no other major contender but had 2 others in this. **Snap Tie** produced the sort of performance his reputation suggested he had in him, in mid-field when hitting the fifth, making headway under pressure at the next and challenging after 2 out but one paced when making another mistake at the last; he will stay beyond 17f, may have further improvement in him over hurdles and should make at least as good a chaser next season. **Rippling Ring**, who looked very well, was up against much stronger opposition than on his hurdling debut and performed with considerable credit, taking a good hold in a handy position, having every chance when weaving around 2 out and no extra in the straight; he is open to further progress, particularly with the emphasis more on speed than here, and should win more races over hurdles, though it could be he'll do even better switched to fences next season.

4046 Irish Independent Arkle Challenge Trophy Chase (Gr 1) (1) (5yo+) 2m (12) £96,934

3363²	TIDAL BAY (IRE) JHowardJohnson 7-11-7 DenisO'Regan	13/2 6/1	1
3488¹	KRUGUYROVA (FR) CREgerton 5-11-0 (s) APMcCoy	12 9/1	13 2
3690¹	NOLAND PFNicholls 7-11-7 RWalsh	2 7/4f	1½ 3
3745¹	Thyne Again (IRE) WJBurke, Ireland 7-11-7 DNRussell	8/1	nk 4
3482³	Mahogany Blaze (FR) NATwiston-Davies 6-11-7 PJBrennan	10/1	6 5
3488 pu	Moon Over Miami (GER) CJMann 7-11-7 NoelFehily	16 14/1	3½ 6
3639³	Scotsirish (IRE) WPMullins,Ireland 7-11-7 DJCondon	20/1	2½ 7
3488²	Ring The Boss (IRE) PJHobbs 7-11-7 RichardJohnson	10/1	11 8
3183⁴	Marodima (FR) PFNichols 5-11-7 SamThomas	33/1	6 9
3837²	Orpen Wide (IRE) MCChapman 6-11-7 LeeVickers	125/1	27 10
3363¹	Leslingtaylor (IRE) JJQuinn 6-11-7 DougieCostello	20/1	6 11
3639¹	Clopf (IRE) EJO'Grady,Ireland 7-11-7 AJMcNamara	10 11/1	ur
2451 pu	French Accordion (IRE) PaulNolan,Ireland 8-11-7 JCullen	33/1	pu
3706 pu	Premiership (IRE) MScudamore 12-11-7 JamesDavies	400/1	pu

2.35race Andrea & Graham Wylie 14ran 4m03.35

It's been a substandard season so far as the 2m novice chasing division has been concerned, but in stretching right away at the end of a well-run race Tidal Bay separated himself from the rest of the class in no uncertain terms, recording a performance in keeping with those of Moscow Flyer and Azertyuiop a few years back. **Tidal Bay** belied any doubts over his effectiveness at the minimum trip with a high-class performance, increasing his standing as the best novice of the season over any distance and promising more still, racing keenly as he kept close touch and quickening clear in a matter of strides after 4 had been in line jumping the second last, still pulling away at the finish; his tendency to throw in the odd mistake (belted fourth) remains, that the reason he doesn't have a 100% record over fences, but otherwise it's hard to imagine anything beating him again if he races again as a novice, while he wouldn't have to improve much more to reach the top of the tree in open company next season. **Kruguyrova**'s level

of ability looks well established but that detracts in no way from how game and likeable she is and this was another fine effort in the face of her stiffest task to date, going off hard in front, soon back there after an uncharacteristic slow jump at the seventh, and rallying to hold second after looking set to get swallowed up 2 out; she might not be the easiest to place to further advantage in the near future, however, particularly given her mark in handicaps. **Noland** failed to deliver quite all he'd promised after winning 2 lesser events, though he's still worth being positive about for the future, his prep not ideal having picked up a bug between those 2 runs while his sweating up uncharacteristically in the paddock was another negative to his chance, unable to quicken after being upsides the first 2 at the second last; apart from diving at the first his jumping was again impressive, and with 2½m+ likely to suit the Grade 2 novice at Ayr next month could be a good place for him to gain more experience, while he appeals as the type to do well in the likes of the Paddy Power next season.

4047 Smurfit Kappa Champion Hdle Challenge Trophy (Gr 1) (1) (4yo+) 2m110y (8) £205,272

3629¹	KATCHIT (IRE) AKing 5-11-10 RobertThornton	10/1	1
2637¹	OSANA (FR) DEPipe 6-11-10 TomScudamore	5 9/2	1 2
3484²	PUNJABI NJHenderson 5-11-10 BJGeraghty	25/1	5 3
2637⁴	Sublimity (FR) JGCarr,Ireland 8-11-10 (t) PACarberry	7/1	1 4
3371²	Straw Bear (USA) NJGifford 7-11-10 APMcCoy	20/1	8 5
3634¹	Catch Me (GER) EJO'Grady,Ireland 6-11-10 RWalsh	9 10/1	2¼ 6
3371¹	Afsoun (FR) NJHenderson 6-11-10 MickFitzgerald	20 16/1	1½ 7
2921⁵	Farmer Brown (IRE) PatrickHughes,Ireland 7-11-10 DNRussell	50/1	1¼ 8
3372	Kawagino (IRE) JWMullins 8-11-10 WayneKavanagh	200/1	7 9
2767²	Harchibald (FR) NMeade,Ireland 9-11-10 (t) PCarberry	13/2	7 10
3629²	Blythe Knight (IRE) JJQuinn 8-11-10 DougieCostello	50/1	2½ 11
3284⁵	Ebaziyan (IRE) WPMullins,Ireland 7-11-10 DJCondon	33/1	¾ 12
4377	Contraband PaulMurphy 10-11-10 TJDreaper	250/1	dist 13
3284¹	Sizing Europe (IRE) HenrydeBromhead,Ireland 6-11-10 AJMcNamara	9/4 2/1f	26 14
2157	Bobs Pride (IRE) DKWeld,Ireland 6-11-10 DenisO'Regan	66/1	pu

3.15race D S J P Syndicate 15ran 4m08.33

Another year, another substandard Champion Hurdle, with some new names coming to the fore, none of the first 3 having contested the race previously; what made it a race above the humdrum, however, was that it was all about guts, the 2 who fought out the finish showing themselves tremendously game, the winner not for the first time, the rider of the runner-up having stretched the field in the back straight (the tactic the probable main reason for the slower time recorded than in the Supreme), which found out some of the less-hearty contenders; the result might have been otherwise on less testing ground/with a different pace set or had Sizing Europe not appeared to go awry in the straight, and with the top 2m hurdlers pretty much much of a muchness there is still plenty of room at the top for a really good young prospect to come through and clean up; we live in hope. **Katchit**, who really took the eye beforehand, might not be the best Champion Hurdle winner ever but there can have been few more admirable, for he produced yet another extremely genuine effort, responding really well to strong driving after leading 2 out, edging left under pressure but holding on well close home as the runner-up rallied (riders of both first and second received bans for excessive use of the whip); whatever his future prospects, and there must be a slight doubt whether he'll be able to continue to take his races so well as he has, he is a most likeable individual who deserves celebrating for his achievements to date. **Osana** ran a fine race, a really gutsy one too, responding well to pressure once headed 2 out having jumped soundly and forced the pace, showing he was in no way flattered by his win in the International, the winner, runner-up then, just progressing enough to beat him; he has the physique to make a chaser and could well take high rank in 2m novice chases next season, though he could equally continue to be a leading

contender in top 2m hurdles. **Punjabi**, who looked very well, fully confirmed the promise of his Newbury run, the only one of those held up in rear to make a significant impact, keeping on to take third near the finish; he won the Grade 1 juvenile at Punchestown last season and presumably a return visit and a clash with several of these will be on the cards. **Sublimity**, who didn't take the eye and was sweating slightly, went a long way to confirming his Champion Hurdle form from 2007, waited with, making headway going well 3 out and challenging at the next but fading after not fluent at the last, the softer ground looking just to find him out; he may well be a contender again in a year's time, with presumably another light campaign on the cards, though he is set to run at Punchestown at the end of this season first. **Sizing Europe**, who looked very well, looked set to play a big part in the finish when travelling strongly and holding every chance 2 out, but something appeared to go wrong and he was heavily eased before the last, walking over the line; it was later claimed that a back problem offered the most likely explanation and he clearly has the ability to win more races at the highest level.

CHELTENHAM Thu, Mar 13

4066 Royal & SunAlliance Chase (Gr 1) (1) (5yo+) 3m110y (19)
£96,934

3604³	ALBERTAS RUN (IRE) *JonjoO'Neill* 7-11-4 APMcCoy	4/1f	1
3306²	ROLL ALONG (IRE) *CarlLlewellyn* 8-11-4 TimmyMurphy	20/1	4½ 2
3604³	BATTLECRY *NATwiston-Davies* 7-11-4 PJBrennan	25/1	3½ 3
3573¹	Silverburn (IRE) *PFNicholls* 7-11-4 SamThomas	13/2 6/1	3 4
3604²	Air Force One (GER) *CJMann* 6-11-4 NoelFehily	11/2 6/1	13 5
3604⁵	Joe Lively (IRE) *CLTizzard* 9-11-4 JoeTizzard	10 7/1	7 6
3730¹	Oscar Park (IRE) *DWPArbuthnot* 9-11-4 (t) SEDurack	13/2 7/1	11 7
3523¹	Verasi *GLMoore* 7-11-4 (b) PhilipHide	20/1	11 8
3643¹	Pomme Tiepy (FR) *WPMullins,Ireland* 5-10-9 RWalsh	9/2	f
3710ᵖᵘ	Bagan (FR) *CJMann* 9-11-4 TonyDobbin	66/1	pu
3630¹	Starzaan (IRE) *HMorrison* 9-11-4 RobertThornton	8 10/1	pu

1.05race Mr Trevor Hemmings 11ran 6m23.66

An unremarkable renewal, which wasn't particularly representative with the only

Irish challenger crashing out at halfway, though the majority of the top British-trained staying novices were present and some still have potential, not least the winner who again showed a tendency to do little in front; the third and fourth quickened things from the twelfth and that pair and the winner were clear at the top of the hill. **Albertas Run** already had the beating of several of these from the Reynoldstown and became the first winner of that in 35 years to go on and land the SunAlliance, coming back on the bridle once getting to the runner-up 2 out and idling after being ridden ahead approaching the last; he's unbeaten in 4 races at 3m and has more improvement in him, looking the ideal type for the Hennessy further down the line, a race 2 of the last 3 winners of this have landed. **Roll Along** aquitted himself well for one so inexperienced over fences and, while he might have been flattered the get past the third and fourth as they tied up, left the impression he'll prove a better horse still over marathon trips, looking well worth a try in something like the Scottish National, though connections may prefer to wait another year; his jumping isn't a worry on the whole for all he made mistakes at the twelfth and second last, and his pre-race demeanour was encouraging for one who has got worked up.

horse of 2m chasing produced a performance as good as has been seen in this race for many a year as he left him for dead at the end of a well-run race, having the entire field well strung out and recording an excellent time. **Master Minded** met Voy Por Ustedes at level weights this time and beat him all the more impressively, posting a performance that puts him head and shoulders above the 2m chasers of the last 3 years and suggests he'll dominate the division for seasons to come; looking in excellent shape prior to getting warm during the parade, his jumping was exemplary and, after moving on with last year's winner at the top of the hill, he was just nudged along to draw right away after the second last, winning with bags to spare; he's the first 5-y-o to win this race in its 49-year history by the way. **Voy Por Ustedes** looked closely matched with the winner on revised terms from Newbury but found that rival improving far too much, coming well clear with him from the fourth last but barely able to get him off the bridle and left for dead turning in; he looked in excellent condition beforehand but, likeable as he is, his chances of winning more good 2m races seem to depend on whether he can avoid Master Minded.

4068 Seasons Holidays Queen Mother Champion Chase (Gr 1) (1) (5yo+) £176,762   2m (12)

3482 *	MASTER MINDED (FR) *PFNicholls* 5-11-10 RWalsh	11/4 3/1	1
3482 2	VOY POR USTEDES (FR) *AKing* 7-11-10 RobertThornton	5/2f	19 2
3606 4	FAIR ALONG (GER) *PJHobbs* 6-11-10 RichardJohnson	12/1	16 3
3747 ur	Schindlers Hunt (IRE) *DTHughes,Ireland* 8-11-10 (v) PCarberry	33/1	1 4
3400 bd	Newmill (IRE) *JohnJosephMurphy,Ireland* 10-11-10 RMPower	40/1	8 5
3182 2	Twist Magic (FR) *PFNicholls* 6-11-10 SamThomas	11/2 5/1	8 6
3182 *	Tamarinbleu (FR) *DEPipe* 8-11-10 (b) TomScudamore	4 7/2	4 7
3182 3	Mansony (FR) *ALTMoore,Ireland* 9-11-10 DNRussell	16/1	pu

2.20race Mr Clive D. Smith 8ran 3m55.50

A couple of the market leaders might have disappointed but last year's winner was on his game as usual and the up-and-coming

4070 Ladbrokes World Hdle (Gr 1) (1) (4yo+) £142,550   3m (12)

3249 *	INGLIS DREVER *JHowardJohnson* 9-11-10 DenisO'Regan	5/4 11/8f	1
3612 *	KASBAH BLISS (FR) *FDoumen,France* 6-11-10 CPieux	9/1	1 2
3640 2	KAZAL (FR) *EoinGriffin,Ireland* 7-11-10 (s) BJGeraghty	12/1	7 3
3249 2	Blazing Bailey *AKing* 6-11-10 RWalsh	7 13/2	4½ 4
3732 2	My Way de Solzen (FR) *AKing* 8-11-10 (b) RobertThornton	9 15/2	nk 5
3640 2	Aitmatov (GER) *NMeade,Ireland* 7-11-10 (t) PCarberry	33/1	2¾ 6
3612 6	Chief Dan George (IRE) *JamesMoffatt* 8-11-10 (s) BrianHughes	100/1	11 7
3732 5	Flight Leader (IRE) *CLTizzard* 8-11-10 JoeTizzard	100/1	10 8
3612 4	Wichita Lineman (IRE) *JonjoO'Neill* 7-11-10 (s) APMcCoy	12 14/1	1¼ 9
3184 4	Material World *MissSuzySmith* 10-11-3 (ec+t) ColinBolger	100/1	3¾ 10
3249	Sonnyanjoe (IRE) *THogan,Ireland* 10-11-10 (s+t) NoelFehily	50/1	18 11
3284 2	Hardy Eustace (IRE) *DTHughes,Ireland* 11-11-10 (t) CODwyer		5 12
	Lough Derg (FR) *DEPipe* 8-11-10 (v) TomScudamore	14 16/1	6 13
3732 *	Ebaziyan (IRE) *WPMullins,Ireland* 7-11-10 DJCondon	20/1	15 14
4047	Redemption *NATwiston-Davies* 13-11-10 DavidEngland	66/1	13 15
3249	Special Envoy (FR) *PBowen* 6-11-10 PJBrennan	250/1	pu
3612 pu	The Market Man (NZ) *NJHenderson* 8-11-10 MickFitzgerald	50/1	pu
3373 2		18 16/1	pu

3.30race Andrea & Graham Wylie 17ran 5m52.88

Normally the feature event on the third day of the Festival, in terms of performance this was somewhat eclipsed by Master Minded's victory in the Champion Chase on this extraordinary day, but this was still a classic race, the best staying hurdlers continuing to show themselves superior to the best 2-milers, the short-priced favourite made to work by a progressive younger rival; the pace was sound, ensuring a proper test of stamina, and there were few excuses for those beaten; due to the previous day's abandonment, the race was run on the Old rather than the New Course, with the start early on the bend going away from the stands. **Inglis Drever**, who for him looked in really good shape, added a third success in this race to his superb tally, improving on the form of his previous wins, producing the best performance over hurdles of the season and displaying all the qualities that have made him such a grand servant to connections over the years; held up jumping well, he made his effort when not having much room before 3 out and responded well to pressure to chase the leaders into the straight, leading after the last and battling on gamely as the runner-up stuck on well; he has seldom been seen to best advantage at Aintree and may be vulnerable if he goes there again, while there has also been talk of his being retired; let's hope he isn't just yet. **Kasbah Bliss**, who looked very well and was led round by 2 attendants, has clearly progressed this year, showing more stamina than previously, and followed his ready win at Haydock with his best-ever performance, making headway going well 3 out, leading after the next and keeping on after a mistake at the last and being headed on the run-in, his rider suspended for excessive use of the whip; he's in

prime position to take over the mantle of the winner should he be retired or age take its toll. **Kazal** ran better than he ever had, having no problem with a truly-run 3m on less testing ground, racing prominently, leading 3 out but headed after the next and no extra from the last; he may be tried again over fences next season but in the shorter term he is likely to be a leading candidate for the Champion Stayers' at Punchestown, given the first 2 are unlikely runners in that.

CHELTENHAM Fri, Mar 14

4082 **Ballymore Properties Nov Hdle** 2½m110y (10)
(Baring Bingham) (Gr 1) (1) (4yo+) £68,424

3565	FIVEFORTHREE (IRE) WPMullins,Ireland 6-11-7 RWalsh	7/1	1	
3065	VENALMAR MFMorris,Ireland 6-11-7 PWFlood	12 11/1	nk 2	
3065	TRAFFORD LAD ESheehy,Ireland 6-11-7 TomDoyle	8 9/1	4 3	
3515	Forpadydeplasterer (IRE) ThomasCooper,Ireland 6-11-7 DNRussell		1 4	
3494	Group Captain AKing 6-11-7 RobertThornton	5 13/2		
3676	Lightning Strike (GER) MissVenetiaWilliams 5-11-7 TomScudamore	9/2 5/1	¾ 5	
		33/1	2 6	
3244	Razor Royale (IRE) NATwiston-Davies 6-11-7 PJBrennan	25 18/1	9 7	
3659	Fond of A Drop DTHughes,Ireland 7-11-7 BJGeraghty	33/1	20 8	
3676	Hold Em (IRE) WKGoldsworthy 6-11-7 TimmyMurphy	33 18/1	5 9	
3039	Breedsbreeze (IRE) PFNicholls 6-11-7 SamThomas	8 9/1	13 10	
3746	Raven's Run (IRE) MichaelCunningham,Ireland 6-11-7 MichaelDarcy		5 11	
2848	Majestic Concorde (IRE) DKWeld,Ireland 5-11-7 PCarberry	66/1		
3244	Aigle d'Or NJHenderson 5-11-7 APMcCoy	33/1	13 12	
3829	King In Waiting (IRE) ADBrown 5-11-7 JasonMaguire	9/2 4/11	7 13	
3515	Whatuthink (IRE) OliverMcKiernan,Ireland 6-11-7 CO'Dwyer	200/1	pu	
		20 14/1	pu	

1.05race Olde Crowbars Syndicate 15ran 5m02.19

The market favoured the British-trained ex-Flat horses over the Irish-trained jumping breds but the latter came firmly to the fore, taking the first 4 places; although there were a couple of notable disappointments and even the best of the home team Group Captain ran a flat race, the form looks well up to recent standards for the event, which continues to hold its own despite the introduction of the Spa, run as a Grade 1 for the first time this year; the pace wasn't at all strong early on but picked up from halfway. **Fiveforthree**, who is still rather unfurnished, showed considerable improvement stepped up in trip on just his second start over hurdles, very confidently ridden, coming through into the straight to lead narrowly at the last and holding on all out; he had quite a hard race but there is more to come, particularly over further, and if he does fill out he promises to make an even better chaser than hurdler. **Venalmar**, a strapping prospective chaser, continued his excellent progress as a hurdler, putting up a smart effort, impressing with the way he travelled through the race, leading before 2 out and having a tremendous battle with the winner on the run-in; he's an exciting prospect for when he goes over fences and will be at least as effective at 3m. **Trafford Lad**, who looked very well, was entitled to beat the second on their running last time but though he ran well that rival progressed more; he was always handy, challenged from 2 out and had every chance at the last but couldn't quicken; he will be at least as effective over further and it would be no surprise to see him back here in a year's time as a leading SunAlliance Chase candidate. **Forpadydeplasterer**, who looked very well, is yet another prospective chaser from the Irish team who showed improved form in this race, held up taking a good hold, making headway and a mistake 2 out and challenging before the last; he was stepping up in trip but didn't appear to have any problem with it, indeed is likely to stay further.

4084 JCB Triumph Hdle (Gr 1) (1) (4yo) £68,424   2m1f (8)

3364²	CELESTIAL HALO (IRE) *PFNicholls* 4-11-0 (t) RWalsh	5/1	1
3248¹	FRANCHOEK (IRE) *AKing* 4-11-0 APMcCoy	5/4 1/1f 2¼	2
3513²	WON IN THE DARK (IRE) *Sabrina,JoanHarty,Ireland* 4-11-0 AJMcNamara	16/1	3
3441¹	Songe (FR) *CELongsdon* 4-11-0 TomSiddall	25/1 4½	4
3760²	Star of Angels *DEPipe* 4-11-0 (b) TomScudamore	50/1 2¼	5
3611¹	Serabad (FR) *PBowen* 4-11-0 (s) PJBrennan	20 14/1 ¾	6
3513¹	Personal Column *MrsJHarrington,Ireland* 4-11-0 BJGeraghty	14 18/1 2	7
3985⁵	Callisto Moon *IanWilliams* 4-11-0 SEDurack	100/1 5	8
3737⁶	Temlett (IRE) *WPMullins,Ireland* 4-11-0 DJCondon	100/1 9	9
3737²	Silverhand (IRE) *NMeade,Ireland* 4-11-0 PCarberry	14 12/1 ¾	10
3484	Five Dream (FR) *PFNicholls* 4-11-0 (b) SamThomas	8 9/1 6	11
3711	Special Day (FR) *MrsLWadham* 4-11-0 DominicElsworth	100/1 17	12
3737³	Beau Michael *AdrianMcGuinness,Ireland* 4-11-0 DNRussell	10/1 3	13
4045	Lemon Silk (IRE) *KJBurke* 4-11-0 (s) PCO'Neill	100/1	pu

2.15race The Stewart Family 14ran 4m07.68

The smallest field for the Triumph since Connaught Ranger was successful in 1978, seemingly indicative of the growing prestige of the Festival's juvenile handicap, and it was a weak renewal overall, hardly any having shown form good enough to even reach the frame in most runnings and the one that certainly had, Franchoek, coming unstuck as things didn't quite go his way; the first 2 home in the Fred Winter ran to a higher level than Celestial Halo as it turned out. **Celestial Halo** fully confirmed the promise of his Newbury win at the second attempt and, whilst the run of the race suited him more than the second, his turn of foot proving decisive turning in after Franchoek had taken longer than expected to press on with him, there are grounds for thinking he can uphold the form if the pair meet at Aintree all the same, with further improvement highly likely and that sort of track likely to play to his strengths more than Franchoek's; he has the potential to go a fair bit further yet, smart on the Flat and looking a much more polished jumper here, ducking right approaching the last but proving most genuine under pressure as he held on. **Franchoek** would have won and, in the process, delivered what his hitherto superb juvenile season had for so long promised had he merely repeated his Finesse form, but circumstances prevented him from doing so against a speedier type; he was content to track the winner instead of making use of his proven stamina, pressing him only 2 out by which time speed was crucial, and though he stuck to his task in typically game fashion he couldn't quite peg him back; he won't be long resuming winning ways, but further improvement seems likely to come at 2½m now. **Won In The Dark** isn't straightforward, but it was impossible to fault him on that score here and this strong-travelling type found still more improvement, sustaining his challenge well without ever looking like getting to the first 2; he's useful now.

4086	totesport Cheltenham Gold Cup Chase (Gr 1)	3¼m110y (22)		
	(1) (5yo+) £268,279			
3483 ¹	DENMAN (IRE) *PFNicholls* 8-11-10 SamThomas	2 9/4		1
3606 ²	KAUTO STAR (FR) *PFNicholls* 8-11-10 (t) RWalsh	1/1 10/11f	7	2
3628 ³	NEPTUNE COLLONGES (FR) *PFNicholls* 7-11-10		sh	3
	MickFitzgerald	25/1		
2828 ²	Halcon Genelardais (FR) *AKing* 8-11-10 RobertThornton	16/1	9	4
2768 ³	Exotic Dancer (FR) *JonjoO'Neill* 8-11-10 (s) APMcCoy	9 17/2	16	5
3247 ⁴	Knowhere (IRE) *NATwiston-Davies* 10-11-10 PJBrennan	25/1	16	6
3741 ⁵	Afistfullofdollars (IRE) *NMeade,Ireland* 10-11-10 PCarberry	20/1	dist	7
3293	Azulejo (FR) *MScudamore* 10-11-10 TomScudamore	200/1		pu
3483 ³	Celestial Gold (IRE) *DEPipe* 10-11-10 TimmyMurphy	100/1		pu
4047	Contraband *PaulMurphy* 10-11-10 TJDreaper	200/1		pu
	Fustrien du Paon (FR) *RichardChotard,France* 12-11-10 (t)			pu
	ALecordier	250/1		
3710 ᵖᵘ	Iron Man (FR) *PBowen* 7-11-10 (s) DenisO'Regan	100/1		pu

3.30race Mr Paul K Barber & Mrs M Findlay 12ran 6m48.02

The most eagerly anticipated Gold Cup of modern times brought with it a huge publicity drive as the 2 stablemates who've dominated the chasing scene since winning this and the SunAlliance last season clashed for the first time; in a race where the dead wood was dropped early on, Denman returned the best Gold Cup performance in over 10 years as he galloped his rivals into submission, though it wasn't the all resolving contest it might have been with Kauto Star not at his best; while Paul Nicholls' 1-2-3 doesn't quite match Michael Dickinson's 'Famous Five' of 1983 it further highlighted the dominance of his stable in jump racing at the moment, a day on from Master Minded's hammer blow in the Champion Chase and cementing his third trainers' title at the meeting on the bounce. **Denman** put up a performance at least as good as in the Hennessy Gold Cup in registering his thirteenth win from 14 starts (only defeat in SunAlliance Hurdle), never looking in any danger after jumping on at the eleventh and galloping on relentlessly as he brushed through 4 out and the next, 12 lengths clear at the second last before tiring a little on the run-

in; his task was undoubtedly made easier by Kauto Star's underperforming and the issue of who's the better horse has still to be resolved, but that makes for an enthralling 2008/9. **Kauto Star** came off worse with his stablemate as he relinquished his Gold Cup crown but didn't seem at his best, failing to jump with his usual fluency and beaten from the fourth last, making hard work of even getting past the third 2 out and then all out to hold that rival's renewed challenge; it can be argued his form is still better than that of Denman and it's to be hoped he's given the chance to exact revenge next season. **Neptune Collonges** pushed an admittedly below-par Kauto Star hard for the runner-up spot and has clearly developed into a top-class chaser himself this season, improving again as he stuck with Denman until 4 out and almost getting back up for second at the death; he'll hold strong claims of landing another Punchestown Guinness Gold Cup, being a much better horse now than last year.

Timeform's Guide To The Tote/Racing Post 'Ten To Follow' Competition

The popularity of National Hunt racing seems at an all-time high. Whilst the powers that be have been obliged to consider the introduction of the so-called 'Sovereign Series', which will bring together ten Group 1 races, to engender a greater level of interest in Flat racing, the 2007/8 jumps season was characterised by thrilling racing and intense debate. The air of anticipation for the season that follows is palpable, and that is likely to be seen in the weight of entries for the Tote's 'Ten To Follow' contest. The contrast between the prize money on offer for the National Hunt and Flat competitions emphasises the relative lure of the former. There was a guaranteed pool of £1 million in the latest season and a first prize—won by Gerry Paulus of Dorset—of £455,000. The winner of the 2008 Flat event receives the relatively paltry sum of £95,955. With so many taking part it may be tempting to look beyond the obvious in order to get an edge. However, it doesn't tend to pay to do so, the most obvious horses the ones who are likely to accumulate most points.

To reinforce this point we need do no more than take a look at last season's leading selections. All of the top ten entries in the competition contained Timeform's top-rated chaser **Kauto Star**, his Gold Cup conqueror, **Denman**, leading staying hurdler **Inglis Drever** and the outstanding novice **Tidal Bay**. In addition all bar one of the lists included **Katchit**, winner of the Champion Hurdle. The first two-named would have been the first two names on the teamsheet this time round, too, but for the concerns which have emerged regarding Denman's irregular heartbeat which will reportedly see him miss the Hennessy in all likelihood. Kauto Star may have lost the aura of invincibility he attained in 2006/7, but at the same time his performances in winning three times, notably when routing the King George field for the second year running, showed him to be as good as ever. He's likely to follow a similar path this season, kept away from stable-companion Denman until March, which means that he's likely to prove an invaluable points earner throughout the campaign. Denman forged a massive reputation for himself last season, extending his unbeaten run over fences to nine, on the final occasion running and jumping his rivals ragged in a Gold Cup that was one of the most eagerly-anticipated of modern times.

Whilst his questionable well-being dictates that he'd be a risky selection at this point, he must be considered as a potential substitute supposing that all is well with him by the turn of the year. Even from a mark of 182, Denman would likely have been favourite for the Hennessy, and in his anticipated absence the race seems sure to have a more open look to it, with plenty more running from in the handicap. **Snowy Morning** was sent off favourite for last year's renewal, yet got no further than the seventh in a race Denman dominated. However, his season thereafter proved a successful one, winning twice over hurdles before finishing placed in competitive chases on his final four starts. The most notable of those efforts were when third in the Grand National and runner-up in the Punchestown Guinness Gold Cup. It could be that there's more to come from Willie Mullins' chaser and he appeals as one who can prove competitive in several of the top chases, including some of those all-important bonus races for which additional points are earned.

Last season's bonus race format was weighted quite heavily in favour of staying chasers, with nine of the fifteen races being chases in excess of two and a half miles, so it makes sense for your ten to follow list to be similarly biased. Tidal Bay stamped himself a novice chaser of the highest quality in completing the Cheltenham/Aintree double and looks one to stick with this time round, too. Concerns regarding his jumping were made to look laughable in the Arkle where he put up a dominating display, and the likelihood is that he's going to prove suited by a step up in trip this season—it would be no surprise to see him starting off in the Old Roan Chase at Aintree. That race arrives before the deadline for entries and, therefore, no final decision about his inclusion will need to be made until then, but if he comes through that test okay he's likely to be worthy of respect in all the top races he contests and to pick up a useful haul of points. Last season's staying novice chasers looked an unremarkable bunch on balance, the winner of the Royal & SunAlliance Chase, **Albertas Run**, subsequently having his colours lowered at Aintree and appearing to have an awful lot to find if he's to successfully mix it with the likes of Kauto Star and Denman.

There had been reports before Inglis Drever won the World Hurdle for a record third time that he would be retired at the end of the season. However, it now seems that he will remain in training in a bid to win a fourth title (no horse had previously won the race more than twice), and whilst his outstanding career record may mark him out as an obvious candidate for a ten to follow list, there are reasons for leaving him out this time. Admittedly, there were no signs of his powers being on the wane during 2007/8—indeed his Cheltenham Festival success was arguably a career-best effort—but he will be ten come next March, and there are a couple of younger rivals likely to be snapping at his heels. The most obvious of those is **Kasbah Bliss**, who ran Inglis Drever to a length, the pair, in turn, seven lengths clear of Kazal at Prestbury Park. That performance proved two things: namely, at the age of six, that Kasbah Bliss remains on the upgrade and that he has no problem getting up the Cheltenham hill—an ability many had doubted beforehand. Being trained by Francois Doumen in France, there's a chance that Kasbah Bliss could be kept to race at Auteuil rather than racking up the points in Britain. However, that seems unlikely in light of the way Doumen has campaigned Baracouda, as well as Kasbah Bliss, which is to say that he's rarely one to miss the opportunity to cross the Channel in search of decent prizes and it's fair to assume that, as last season, the Long Distance, Long Walk and Rendlesham will all be on the agenda. He's shown his well-being on the Flat in 2008 and looks one of the stand-out favourites for Cheltenham, even at this very early stage. Other staying hurdlers to consider are **Blazing Bailey** and three who'll be having their first season out of novice company, **Elusive Dream**, **Whiteoak** and **Franchoek**. Blazing Bailey is admirably tough, as he demonstrated by winning at Aintree and Punchestown having finished fourth in the World Hurdle, though he's fairly well exposed and the suspicion is that Kasbah Bliss is that bit better. The three novices mentioned filled the first three places in the Mersey Novices' Hurdle at Aintree, Elusive Dream rather getting first run on the placed horses, all showing themselves to be smart recruits. Elusive Dream enjoyed a fine first season over hurdles and could well do better still, though it's possible that he'll not have the mid-winter opportunities of some of the others given that he seems unsuited by testing conditions. The advantage of siding with Whiteoak is that she's likely to prove capable of plundering some of the newly-established mares races as well as being competitive against the males. She seems versatile with regards trip and, although yet to be tried, is likely to stay three miles. Franchoek has also yet to race over three miles, though his stamina looks nigh-on assured, arguably inconvenienced by not having enough use made of him when second to Celestial Halo in the Triumph Hurdle and when third at Aintree.

The two-mile hurdling division probably holds more potential champions than any other. Katchit is an admirably consistent performer, though rated as no more than an average winner of the Champion Hurdle, with arguably both **Sizing Europe** and **Sublimity** shaping better than the winner. Sizing Europe looked a serious Champion Hurdle candidate when winning the Greatwood in atrocious conditions at Cheltenham's Open meeting and then, more impressively still, the AIG Europe Champion Hurdle at Leopardstown in

January. A horse of substance, Sizing Europe looks a chaser of the future, though the manner in which he travelled until patently suffering a problem in the Champion Hurdle would suggest he's worth keeping to hurdles for the time being (which seems likely at the time of writing). Either way, there look to be numerous opportunities for Sizing Europe, particularly as his Cheltenham capitulation will hopefully prove to be a one-off. Like Sizing Europe, Sublimity impressed with the way in which he travelled through the Champion Hurdle, only for him seemingly to find the unusually testing conditions counting against him from the bottom of the hill. In finishing fourth he did enough to show that his success twelve months earlier was no fluke, confirming himself a serious challenger for next year's rendition, too. Supporters of the 2007 champion are entering the unknown to some degree, however, as his owner Bill Hennessy has moved his charge away from the care of John Carr to that of his son, and rookie trainer, Robbie. **Osana** ran a fine race to finish runner-up to Katchit at Cheltenham and the advantage of selecting David Pipe's charge is that not only has he proved himself capable of mixing it at the top level over hurdles but he remains with the potential to do just as well over fences. Of those graduating from novice company **Jered** and **Binocular** both gave the impression that they'd be up to making their mark against Katchit & co this season. Even if his performances to date have more style than substance to them, Jered can confidently be expected to make into one of the leading contenders for the Champion Hurdle; he impressed more and more throughout his novice season, which culminated with a facile success in the Champion Novices' at Punchestown. He's yet to be tested outside of Ireland, though it's worth bearing in mind that the calendar throws up a plethora of races in his homeland and he'll likely be able to rack up the points without crossing the Irish Sea until Cheltenham. Binocular made massive strides in a short space of time last season, his sole defeat coming when just edged out by **Captain Cee Bee** in the Supreme Novices' Hurdle at the Festival. He was well suited by the greater test of speed when gaining compensation at Aintree three weeks later, showing himself a juvenile of the highest order in beating the Triumph Hurdle winner, **Celestial Halo**, comfortably. He's an edgy type who tends to get on his toes and sweat up, so there's a slight fear that he could get overwhelmed on the biggest of occasions, though it hasn't stopped him so far and that's only a slight negative for a horse who otherwise is all positive.

Finding the winner of the 2008/9 Champion Chase seems to pose less of a problem. Such was the magnitude of **Master Minded**'s success at Cheltenham

Binocular (near side) should be a useful points scorer in the top two-mile hurdles

that his subsequent Aintree defeat—over two and a half miles—is readily banished from thoughts when considering the two-mile division. It surely would be folly to omit a horse who rose to prominence with such blinding effect from any list. Back at the minimum trip it's easy to picture him winning the Tingle Creek at Sandown—where he's already proved his effectiveness—before going on to confirm himself the best around at the minimum trip. In truth there's little alternative to him; Tidal Bay seems sure to prove better suited by a stiffer test of stamina, whereas the reliable **Voy Por Ustedes,** for all he got his revenge on Master Minded at Aintree, is reportedly due to be campaigned over further from now on. Given that the Champion Chase is the only two-mile chase granted 'bonus' status, there's little reason to consider entering more than one specialist at that trip in one's list. Perhaps Master Minded's most formidable rival will be **Well Chief,** who's reportedly on the road back having missed out last season. His problems dictate that he's an extremely risky pick, however.

Arguably it's the handicaps that win the competition, and finding suitable contenders for them is far harder. We will have a fair idea of those horses who are likely to be to the fore of the betting for the Paddy Power at Cheltenham (and perhaps the Hennessy at Newbury) before the entry deadline, though beyond that it's harder to judge the make-up of the top handicaps. **Bible Lord** appeals as one who could prove a leading player for the first-named event, sure to take advantage of a mark (136) that looks to underplay his ability at some stage, so long as he cuts out a tendency to make mistakes, something which hindered him last season. Another who appeals as the sort to win another big handicap, also amongst the fifty, is **An Accordion**. Whilst the latest running of the William Hill Trophy at Cheltenham in March wasn't anything like as competitive as can be the case, An Accordion looked to have more in hand than the margin of his success suggested, not for the first time appearing to do only as much as was necessary on getting to the front. As such, it would be no surprise to see him raise his game again, to the extent that a 9 lb rise could well prove lenient. The Hennessy could well be on the agenda for him, as it is likely to be for his stablemate and 2008 Grand National winner, **Comply Or Die**. Rated 154, he's 2 lb higher than An Accordion, and whilst it's a bit more of a stretch to see him getting involved in some of the big handicaps prior to Aintree, he took so well to the Grand National fences that he's worth considering with a view to that race alone. He's possibly one to draft in at the substitute stage so as to have him on side come the big race in April.

In perming entries it's important to try and get the right combinations, with the emphasis placed in the right areas. As we've found it pays to be 'staying chaser-heavy', whilst incorporating a horse or two in each of the remaining divisions. Kauto Star should be penned in in bold and underlined in triplicate and, along with him, Tidal Bay, An Accordion and Snowy Morning would make up the first four places in our entry. Master Minded is impossible to omit and Kasbah Bliss makes a little more appeal than Inglis Drever as our World Hurdle hope. Sizing Europe, Jered and Binocular are handy additions on the basis that they all have the option of fences should things not go to plan in their hurdling campaigns. The final 'wild card' position goes to Bible Lord. Perms could be made up with the likes of Franchoek, Whiteoak and Osana. It would be dangerous to select Denman at this stage given doubts surrounding his health, but if it transpires that all is sound he looks a banker for drafting in during the transfer window in January.

Index

Index